Audio Editing with

Adobe Audition

Richard Riley

PC Publishing
Keeper's House
Merton
Thetford
Norfolk IP25 6QH
UK

Tel 01953 889900
Fax 01953 889901
email info@pc-publishing.com
web site http://www.pc-publishing.com

First published 2004

© PC Publishing

ISBN 1 870775 94 5

British Library Cataloguing in Publication Data
A catalogue record for this book is available from the British Library

Cover design by Hilary Norman Design

Printed and bound in Great Britain by Biddles, Kings Lynn, Norfolk

Introduction

In May 2003 Adobe Systems Incorporated acquired Cool Edit Pro; the pro PC audio editing software product developed by Syntrillium Corp. In August of the same year Adobe reintroduced Cool Edit Pro to the market as Adobe Audition. This move enabled Adobe to offer a high quality audio editing tool alongside the state of the art suite of imaging and digital video products already in development. After the sale, Syntrillium immediately dropped completely out of sight along with the enormous amount of resources, forums and knowledge bases that had grown up alongside Cool Edit and Cool Edit Pro during the lifetime of the product from 1996 to 2003. The loss of these resources is unfortunate for anyone new to Adobe Audition and deserves mention. This book aims to help fill this gap by adding to the extraordinarily well written and informative on-line help (much of it written by the original developers) through providing step through guides to complex tasks like creating a multitrack recording or preparing a finished soundtrack for a movie.

Some of the content of this book was first published in 2002 as *Audio Editing with Cool Edit,* and I hope that I can provide help to newcomers to Adobe Audition by revising my original copy to suit the new release. This also presents me with an opportunity to include even more information in this new book, particularly in the areas of combining audio with movies and MIDI files, loops and shortcuts etc. Most of the original copy has been rewritten for Adobe Audition along with new grabs and an emphasis on Audition interacting with other Adobe products.

My thanks to all at Syntrillium for their help with the first release. Extra special thanks to Phil Chapman and his fabulous expanding deadline, and most of all to Jo Riley without whom this book would never have been finished – again.

Contents

Introduction to Adobe Audition

Adobe Audition waveform recording and editing program for the PC enables advanced and non-advanced PC users to compose and produce complete audio soundtracks using waveform editing tools to perform simple and complex editing and audio shaping tasks. Adobe Audition also has the ability to render hundreds of waveforms into a single stereo waveform in real time. This enables Adobe Audition to be used as a virtual recording and production studio. Adobe Audition contains effects and other tools to enhance waveform playback and is able to encode very high quality audio into movie soundtracks for the creation of DVD's and other media. For home users, archivists, musicologists and technicians the advanced noise reduction and clean up tools enable recovering and archiving of precious vinyl records or any recorded sound source. Music production and mastering, creating MP3 files for the web, recording waveforms for sample players and producing jingles for radio shows are just some of the complex tasks you can easily complete using this software.

Installation

Adobe Audition requires little technical effort to perform a successful installation. In most cases it is enough to follow the defaults. If you experience any difficulties running Adobe Audition successfully please consult the chapter 'Troubleshooting and Advanced Configuration' at the end of the book.

Step 1

Run the installation program 'Setup.exe' from CD or other media. This 'splash' screen will appear. Press 'Next' at the splash screen to start the installation.

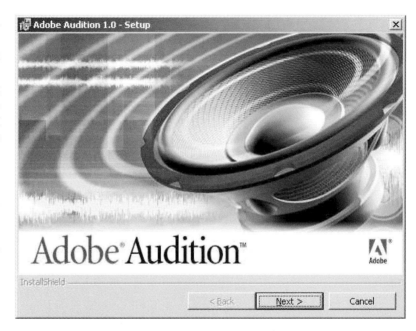

Step 2

Press next to confirm and continue the installation.

Continue the installation

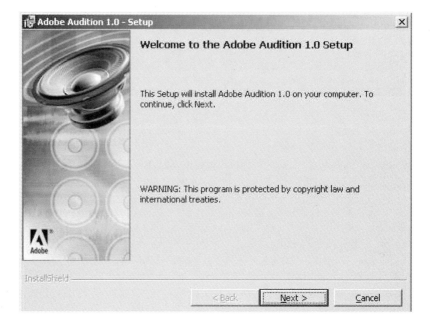

Step3

Select your language preference for the End User License Agreement (EULA).

Select your language preference

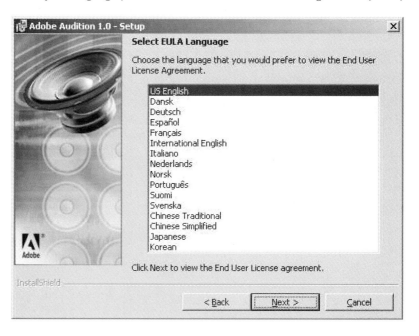

Step 4

Press 'Next' to confirm your acceptance of the license agreement.

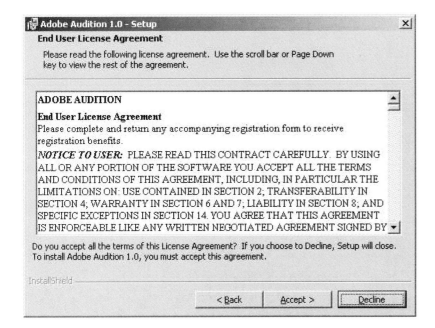

Confirm your acceptance of the license agreement

Step 5

Enter your name and other details if you wish. The serial number is necessary as the installation cannot continue without a valid serial number. The number is printed on the inside cover of the Adobe manual or on the CD Jewel Case.

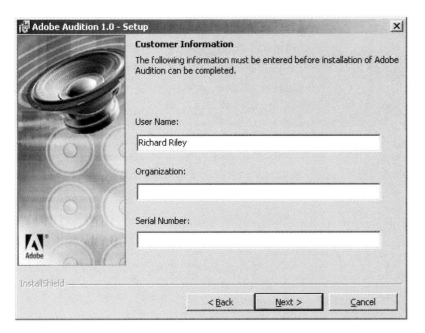

Enter your name and other details

Step 6

Registered users of Cool Edit Pro may download Adobe Audition free of charge from Adobe.com. The upgrade serial number that is available from the same place will only allow you to install the software if you have installed a registered version of Cool Edit Pro on the same PC. The software will install alongside Cool Edit Pro therefore it is not necessary to uninstall Cool Edit Pro in advance of installing Adobe Audition.

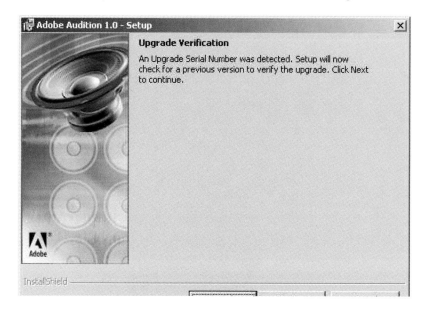

Step 7

Confirm your acceptance of the default location for the program files or choose another. It is acceptable to install away from your system or boot device if you are running short on space. Note. This is not the location for your audio files and sessions.

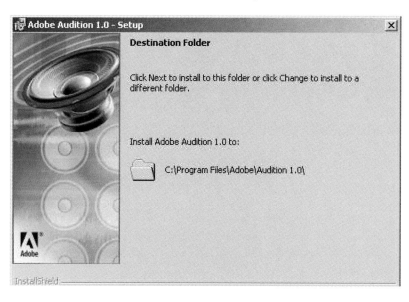

Step 8

Adobe Audition is packaged with a number of filters enabling the software to decode and encode in a variety of formats. The default is for just a selection of filters to be installed. However if you later decide that additional filters are necessary it is not possible to install the missing filters from within the program. Therefore install the entire selection of filters and reset file associations for other programs at another time if necessary.

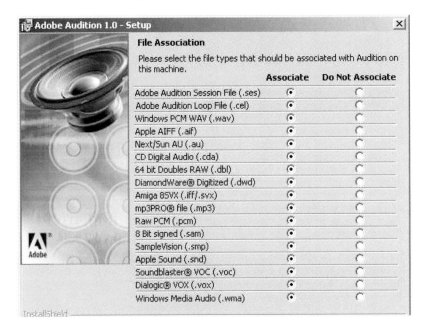

Install the entire selection of filters

Step 9

Press Install to install the program files.

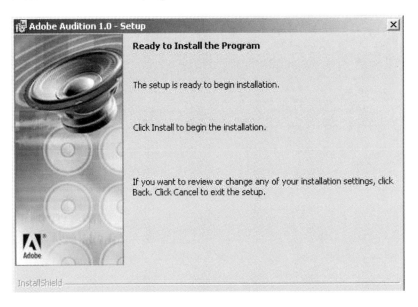

Install the program files

Step 10

Wait while the files are installed.

Wait while the files are installed

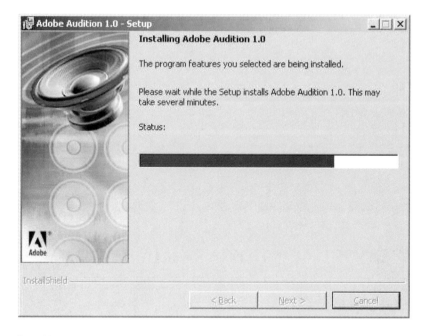

Step 11

Congratulations! You have successfully installed Adobe Audition.

Setup completed

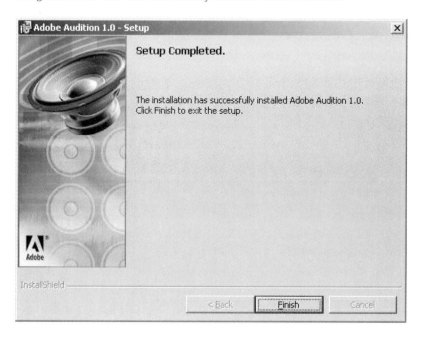

Running Adobe Audition for the first time

Prepare your system by closing any programs that are not being used immediately. The operating system will enable other programs to be run in the background but you will find that performance is noticeably enhanced if Adobe Audition is running alone, especially when managing a large Adobe multitrack session.

Starting the program

From the Windows Start Button choose Programs > Adobe Audition.

The first time Adobe Audition is started you will see a message prompting you to confirm the default choice of location for temporary files. These files can be very large. By default Adobe Audition will choose your physical device with the largest amount of free space. This is normally fine and you may press OK to agree. If your PC contains a physical disk with a great deal of free space you may wish to choose a smaller disk with a faster data access time. If you press 'No' the program will start and you will have to manually choose an alternative location.

Tip

Programs are installed with the last one right at the bottom of the list. This can be inconvenient if you have installed a lot of programs. You can sort the program names if you wish by right clicking over any program name within the list and choosing 'Sort By Name' from the menu.

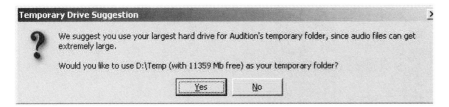

You will see a message prompting you to confirm the default choice of location for temporary files

Choosing an alternative location for temporary files

From the menu bar choose 'Options' then 'Settings'. From within the Settings dialog choose the 'System' tab to reveal the following options.

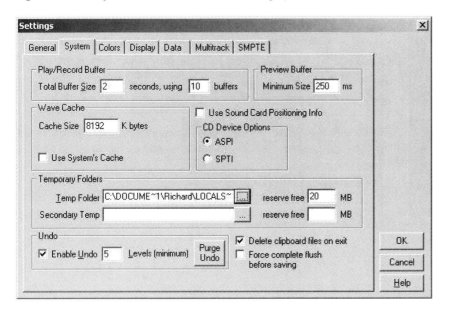

You will see a message prompting you to confirm the default choice of location for temporary files

Tip

The settings dialog may be revealed at any time by pressing the F4 button on your keyboard.

If you choose not to accept the alternative, Adobe Audition will default to your home folder for temporary files. Even though these are deleted after every successful shutdown there may still be an issue for you if you have disk quotas enabled or are working on a corporate LAN. For safety it is recommended that you choose an alternative high speed storage device inside your PC with enough free space (at least 1GB). The temporary files folder should also not be used for any other data although it may be a folder within a folder tree such as your system partition etc. Use the button on the right of the file path to browse to an alternate location.

A quick start guide to Adobe Audition

This chapter introduces the tools and features you will need to quickly create soundtracks for use on their own or as a soundtrack to your movies. Sound captured by Adobe Audition is always displayed in visual form. The visual interpretation of the sound is called a waveform. Editing is performed on the waveform and the results are reproduced through the sound card as the playback cursor moves over the waveform on screen.

Instant gratification

Later on in this book is an advanced guide to the inner functions of this important software. But if all you want to do is get on with creating your soundtracks and sort the rest out later; read on.

- Connect speakers of amplifier to your sound card output.
- Start Adobe Audition
- If not already visible, press F12 to switch to the Multitrack View.
- Drag any wav, mp3 or other audio format file onto any track in the multitrack view.
- Wait for the green mix gauge to finish filling.
- Use the mouse to press the 'play' button on the transport bar.
- Adobe Audition is playing.

Import a movie into Adobe Audition

Movies are viewed in the main Audition workspace called the 'Multitrack View'. Multiple audio files are placed along the length of the movie to create the soundtrack. The multitrack view is an arrange window featuring 'tracks' (like tape tracks) running left to right. Audio files are dropped onto different tracks and are rendered as waveforms that may be cut, muted, looped etc. As the playback cursor moves along the window the waveforms are reproduced as audio. Arrangements can be as long as required, even many hours long. Each track can accommodate either mono or stereo waveforms and has track properties such as volume, pan, tone, effects, etc. One .AVI movie file may be loaded into each Multitrack arrangement. Arrangements are saved as sessions. Loaded waveforms are called waveblocks.

Importing a movie

- Click once inside Track 1 to select it as the target track for the Movie.
- Choose 'Insert' > 'Video From File' from the menu bar and select your .avi movie.
- Press 'Open' to add the movie to your arrangement.

Figure 2.1
Importing a movie

Info

Audition is able to load .avi movies only. Other movie file formats may not be loaded.

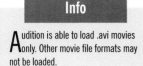

Any existing audio track will be extracted from the movie and rendered as a complete waveform for editing in the Edit View. If the movie already has a soundtrack it must be converted to the frequency rate and bit depth of the current session. If conversion needs to be performed Adobe Audition will present an options dialogue. Choose 32bit 44100hz stereo and dither down to 16bit at mixdown. Effects and envelopes can be added over the waveform in the Multitrack View. The resizable Audition video window will open to show the movie playback. Press the spacebar to see playback. The time display window underneath the arrangement shows elapsed decimal time. Right click within the Time Display choose SMPTE FPS (Frames Per Second). Within the arrangement the movie may be moved backwards and forwards but may not be split. Right click and drag the movie to the beginning of the arrangement for easier management.

Use the transport controls below the arrangement to play, pause and rewind the movie. New users of Audition often comment on the default behaviour. That is, pressing the Play button will start playback but playback will stop once the cursor has reached the end of the viewable range (the extreme right of the window). Use the Play to End control (pictured right) to prevent Audition from pausing playback at the edge of the range.

Add waveforms to your soundtrack

The soundtrack to the movie may be composed of any number of unique wave-forms and waveforms from any source may be used within the arrangement. There are many on-line sources of library music, layers, pads and effects with which you may create a superb soundtrack without ever having to record or even edit your waveforms. Careful positioning of pre-recorded waveblocks is an easy way to create a finished product in very little time. Bass, Middle, Treble and Balance may be adjusted for each track. Reverb or other digital effects may also be added to the audio and dramatic fade in or out effects created using envelopes.

Tip

Try www.sound-effects-library.com for a great range of effects you can use.

Figure 2.2
Add waveforms to your soundtrack.

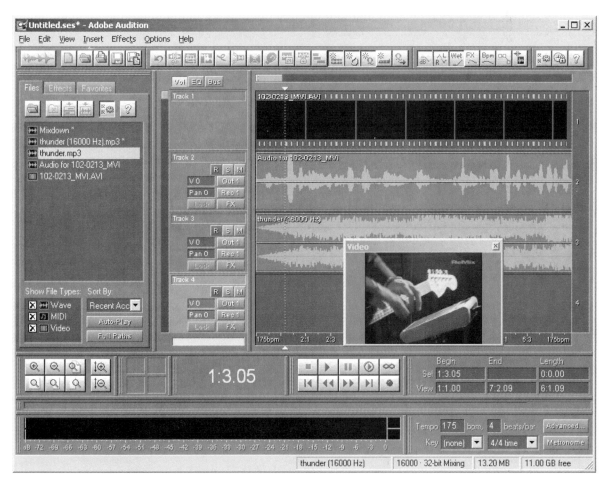

There are a number of ways to add a waveform into an arrangement:

1   Insert>Wave From File from the menu bar.
2   File>Open Waveform from the menu bar.
3   Press Alt + 9 on the keyboard to open the Navigator Window.
4   View the File/Cue list by choosing View>File/Cue List from the menu bar and dragging files directly from this list into the multitrack.
5   Drag any valid file format from the Windows environment directly into a track.

The first file is loaded as a waveform in track one in the Multitrack view. Subsequent waveforms are loaded into tracks two, three, etc. in the order in which they are chosen unless the wave is dragged on the track in which case it will stay where it lands. It's not necessary to label a track as an audio track, nor is it necessary to ensure that only one waveform is able to play at a time. Unlike other audio programs Adobe Audition will render any number of waveforms simultaneously. So it's OK to have waveforms in tracks 1,2,3 and 4 all set to output through the same device. Waveforms appear as green blocks containing the name and an image of the source waveform. Press the spacebar to hear the Multitrack session play but remember to keep an eye on the mix gauge. The session has been completely rendered and is able to play immediately when the mix gauge is green. If the mix gauge is grey the session may still playback although you may experience jumps and skips as the program attempts to render the session in the background.

Press the spacebar to toggle play and stop or use the mouse to play to end or loop any selected range.

Importing audio only from a movie

In the multitrack view choose Insert>Audio From Video File. Adobe Audition will separate the audio from the movie and insert the audio as a waveblock in the first available free track. Any number of AVI soundtracks may be imported into an arrangement.

Moving and copying waveforms

Right click and drag the waveblock forwards or backwards in the arrangement. Press and hold the shift key while right clicking to drag a duplicate image of the block elsewhere. The new image is a ghost of the original and inherits all changes made to the original waveform. However track properties, pan and volume envelopes etc. will not be applied to images in other tracks. In this way one waveform can be made to sound very different on two or more tracks while using the minimum amount of space and resources. Press and hold the control key and then right click and drag any waveblock to a new location in the session to create a brand new copy of any waveform. The copy is a unique waveform and may be edited in the Edit View without changing the original. If the original waveblock has been looped many times (see 'Block Edge Dragging') the new waveform will also be looped. Volume and pan envelopes are also inherited but will only be applied in Multitrack View.

It's not possible to copy track properties ('clone' a track).

Removing and deleting waveforms

Remove any waveform or waveblock from the session by clicking on it to select and pressing the delete key on the keyboard (backspace won't do it). Deleted waveforms remain in the navigator window. Waveforms may be permanently removed from the session if the Backspace key is pressed while holding the Ctrl key (Ctrl + Backspace). This action permanently removes the waveform and all references to it from the session. A dialogue box appears to remind you that this action cannot be undone!

Any number of waveforms may be selected if the keyboard 'control' key (Ctrl) is held while clicking on a new waveform. Waveblocks may be grouped by pressing Ctrl + G on the keyboard or by right clicking over a selected waveblock if two or more waveblocks are selected. Grouped waves may be moved and deleted as one. The colour of the grouped block may be changed by right clicking over any waveblock in the group and choosing group colour from the right click menu. Groups are especially useful for identifying associated waveblocks (waveforms containing a key theme perhaps) in a busy session. From the right click menu grouped waveblocks may also be mixed down to one waveform. Mixing down in this way preserves resources and enables sessions to load and save more efficiently.

Playback cursor, cues and ranges

The playback cursor is always visible on the Multitrack Window. Playback always starts from the cursor position. Clicking inside the arrangement will move the cursor to the mouse position. Playback will then start from midway through the arrangement. To bring the playback cursor to the start of the arrangement press the home key on the keyboard. The playback cursor can also be dragged using the yellow handles above and below the arrangement.

Shuttle

During playback press and hold the left mouse button over either the fast forward or rewind controls to shuttle the cursor manually. Right click to see shuttle options.

Ranges

Left click and drag over the arrangement to create a selection. The playback cursor will now move to the beginning of the selected range. Press the Zoom To Selection button on the transport to expand the range to fill the arrangement window. If the F8 key on the keyboard is pressed additional cursors will appear above and below the arrangement. These indicate a cue range. Ranges will stick until they are deleted and can be named, etc. Double click on the Range name to select the cue range.

Press the 'infinity' button on the transport bar to put Adobe Audition into 'Loop Play' mode.

Cues

Press F8 on the keyboard at any time to create cue points. A basic cue point is a marker that can be used for any function. Cues can be named and used to create a playlist. View>Cue List to see the Cue list. From within this dialog box you can edit and rearrange the cues for the session. Cues can be vital during a complex ses-

sion. Press and hold Shift +F8 to create a track Cue. A track cue is used to identify the start of a new track on a CD. Use track cues to manage a mixdown before
burning to CD. Double click on any cue within the list to have the playback cursor
jump to that position. Cues may also be dragged using the handle above the
arrangement. Right click on the handle to see options for that Cue point.

Snapping

The playback cursor will snap to the nearest waveblock by default. This is convenient when working with waveblocks in the arrangement view. Choose other snapping options from the Edit>Snapping menu. Choose Snap to Ruler (coarse) to
enable snapping to the ruler bar. This is most useful when working with Bars and
Beats.

Lock in Time

You may have discovered the fatal flaw in the Audition session; it's too easy to move a waveblock a few pixels out
of time when simply attempting to edit waveblock properties. This is because right click and drag moves the
block whereas right click produces the useful menu. For this reason always lock each track as soon as the
waveblocks are loaded into the right place. This will also improve system performance. For maximum flexibility lock
each waveblock in time by carefully right clicking over the block and choosing 'Lock In Time' from the menu. This
will allow envelope editing, etc. while ensuring that the waveblock is firmly stuck in time.

Figure 2.3
Lock in time allows envelope editing, etc.
while ensuring that the waveblock is firmly
stuck in time.

Tip

Right click over any image and
choose 'Convert to Unique Copy'
from the drop down menu to create a
new waveform.

Edit undo

Adobe Audition features a minimum of five levels of Undo. In practise this can't always be relied on to rescue your
soundtrack from disaster, especially if your changes included large edits forcing the creation of very large
temporary files. But if you casually deleted half a dozen wave blocks by mistake don't forget to Edit Undo. However
Edit Undo is no substitute for carefully saving your session when things are going well.

Export the soundtrack with the movie

When the multitrack session is complete choose File>Save Mixdown to Video from
the menu bar. Choose a location for the file and press OK. The entire arrangement
minus any muted waveblocks or muted tracks are encoded along the length of the
movie.

Building, layering and producing your original soundtrack

Portions of waveforms lend themselves to being repeated. For instance a solo drum passage will usually contain a steady rhythm two or four beats in length. This rhythm part can be cut from the rest of the passage and looped to form a steady rhythm part which can repeat for as long as you need. 2000 ready made Acrobat loops are distributed with the Audition program files on your Adobe Audition CD. These ready made loops are distributed as CEL files. CEL files are pre-recorded loops containing mp3 encoded waveforms with additional information in the header enabling Adobe Acrobat to correctly place them in an arrangement.

Figure 3.1
Notice the cross hatching in the lower right hand corner of the block. This indicates that block edge dragging is enabled for that block.

Creating a looped passage in your soundtrack
1 Use the files tab in the Navigator pane to browse and select your Cel files.
2 Drag a cel file onto any free track in the arrangement. The cel will be placed at the location of the playback cursor and appears like any other waveblock. A circle icon appears in the corner of the block to indicate that it is set up for looping.
3 Click and drag the over the shaded corner of the waveblock. Drag the edge of the waveblock along the track to set the number of repeats.
4 Press play to hear the repeated loop.

Changing the pace or tempo of your loops
Pre-recorded CEL files are set to match the session tempo of the arrangement. Each CEL will automatically change length to suit the new tempo of the session. Change the tempo using Session Properties from the View menu. Use the metronome button to hear Adobe Audition count time along with the session. The metronome click is an audio click and will appear at the device specified as the Edit View device (the default playback device) in Options>Device Order. It is not possible to produce a MIDI metronome or to dynamically change the tempo or speed

Info

It's much easier to use loops in a session if you choose 'Bars and Beats' from the display time options. Right click over the display time underneath the arrangement to see options.

Figure 3.2
Session Tempo and Metronome are in the
Advanced Session Properties dialog.

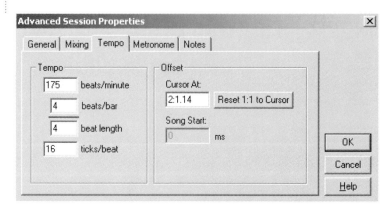

up and slow down the pace of the music using the session tempo feature. Changes made to the session tempo are applied to the entire arrangement globally but do not affect the frame rate of AVI files.

Tip

Choose the infinity symbol on the transport controls to loop a just a section of the arrangement for playback. Playback will loop over a selection of the viewable range. Click and drag between any two points on the ruler bar below the arrangement to select the range.

Change the feel of the soundtrack using volume, tone and digital effects

Properties for volume tone and effects are controlled using track controls at the left of each track in the Multitrack View. Controls for mute, solo and record are placed here along with editable parameters for track EQ, track volume, track pan (balance between left and right) and track FX mix. Changes made to these values affect the entire track. Left click and drag over each field in the track control bar to change volume and pan settings. Use the three buttons marked Vol, EQ and Bus to change view and access further parameters for three-band EQ and Effects Mix. Alternatively drag the right hand side of the track controls bar to see all the controls in one view.

Tip

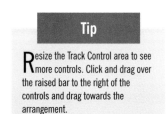

Resize the Track Control area to see more controls. Click and drag over the raised bar to the right of the controls and drag towards the arrangement.

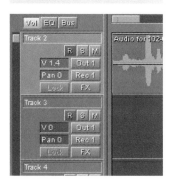

Figure 3.3
Track Controls area showing Pan and Volume controls.

Adjusting volume and pan for a track

Click over the 'V' value in the track controls and vertically drag to cut and boost the level of a track. Do the same over the 'P' value for left / right balance. Alternatively right click to the left of the FX and Lock button to view faders for each. Automated fade and pan effects cannot be made by simply moving these faders. Automated effects are created using envelopes later in this chapter.

Soloing and muting tracks

Any track may be soloed by pressing the yellow 'Solo' button in the track controls bar. Soloing simply mutes every other track than the one being 'soloed'. Press and hold the Control button on the keyboard, then press other 'solo' buttons to hear additional tracks at the same time. Pressing the green 'mute' button will mute tracks and additional tracks by employing the Control key as before.

Naming tracks

To rename any track click once in the track name field and overtype the default name. Moving a wave block between tracks does not change the track name however so if you have a large waveform containing a full length vocal in track two and move the block to track one, track two will still be called 'Vocals'.

Track devices (inputs and outputs)

Each track can be assigned to any sound card device installed in the host computer. Any number of tracks may be assigned to just one pair of outputs. A particular strength of Adobe Audition is the ability of the program to handle multiple wave blocks in different tracks. Audition is not limited to playing back only as many waveforms as you have output devices. A single arrangement may contain up to 128 tracks of audio playing at the same time assigned to just one stereo pair of outputs. Track outputs are assigned using the button marked 'Out 1' in the track properties bar. This button is labelled depending on the target device so could be Out1, Out2 or BusA depending on the selected device. Inputs are assigned in the same way using the button marked 'Rec1'.

To change the order in which devices appear in the Wave Out list, or to remove unused devices from the list choose 'Options'>'Device Order' from the menu bar. All devices installed correctly and enabled inside the computer will appear in the device order

Track EQ (equalisation or tone controls)

Use the EQ button above the track controls to reveal the EQ properties for each track. Place the mouse cursor over any one of the three EQ controls in each of the Track Controls Lo, Mid and Hi. Left click and drag vertically to raise (boost) and lower (cut) the amplitude of each frequency band. Caution these values are in dB. Adding 3dB to each band will raise the overall amplitude of the waveform by nearly 10dB and may cause clipping. Apply EQ sparingly for best results.

Figure 3.4
Track EQ window. A tab is available for each track.

Advanced track EQ

A powerful EQ system for each track is hidden behind the three simple controllers for L (Low) M (Mid) and H (High) EQ in the Track Controls and Track Properties windows. Right click over any of the three controls to reveal the floating Track Equalizers window. The window is resizable by grabbing one corner of the window. In the upper right hand corner (below the Windows title bar) are two small arrows; one pointing left or right and one pointing up or down. Click the left/right arrow to reveal advanced Track Equalisation controls. Using these controls it is possible to apply up to 32dB of boost to any frequency with variable Q. Q is the ratio

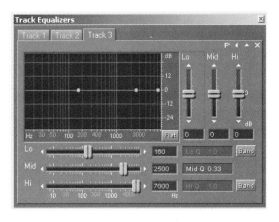

of width to centre frequency. At higher 'Q' the shape of the EQ curve around the centre frequency becomes very sharp allowing for small amounts of boost or cut to be applied to a small frequency band while lower Q settings produce a very wide curve allowing for much softer EQ to be applied. Band pass filters for high and low EQ can also be applied To reset the track EQ to the default settings press the 'Flat' button in the lower right hand corner of the EQ window. The Track Equaliser does not allow for automation, for automated EQ it is necessary to apply the Dynamic EQ effect to the waveform within Edit View. EQ presets may be created and saved using the small P icon in the top right hand corner of the EQ window.

Hint

Both the Track Properties and Track Equaliser windows are floating but can easily be docked with another window. Drag the floating window above or below the multitrack view and drop onto any toolbar. The window will resize itself to fit. Using this technique it is possible to create a very easy to use, yet professional environment allowing 'at a glance' visual indications of track controls and EQ. Simply click on any track to see track properties. To undock a window and return it to a floating state; use the mouse to grab the double handle to the left of the controls in the docked window and drag the window outside of the workspace. It looks really cool if you arrange the workspace so that the track properties, track equalization and level meters are lined up next to each other under the multitrack view. The level meters will 'stand on end' if there's just enough room which looks even more professional.

Add digital effects to a track

Any number of digital effects may be rendered over a waveform. Adobe Audition offers three types of digital effect;

- Real Time Effects. These are non-destructive effects that may be overlaid onto waveforms in the Multitrack View.
- Off Line Effects. These complex effects may only be applied to waveforms in the edit view. Although they are destructive the result of applying the effect may be heard before finally saving the waveform.
- Multitrack Effects. These effects are created using waveforms from two or more tracks in Multitrack View. The result of the effect is created in a mixdown file.

Adding real-time digital effects to any track is as easy as drag and drop

1 Choose the Effects tab from the navigator in Multitrack View
2 Choose 'Group Real-Time Effects' from the two push buttons at the base of the navigator and deselect the option to group by category.
3 Choose a real-time effect and drag over any track.
4 Select preset effect patches or create your own using the faders from within the properties dialog.
5 Choose the level of the effect using the mixers tab from the effects properties. Close the effects properties if you wish.
6 Right click over the FX button from within track controls to see effects options. Left click over the FX button to reveal the effects properties for that track.
7 Drag additional effects over the track to combine effects types.

Advanced digital effects

Each track in the multitrack view can be routed through a 'rack' of real time soft-ware effects such as reverb or delay. Adobe Audition comes with a hundred or so effects. Not all effects are enabled right away. You much choose which effects to use on the track and place them in a virtual effects rack. The track is automatical-ly routed through the rack on playback. Each track may have an effects rack how-ever care must be taken as effects impose an enormous load on the processor and are frequently unstable. If you have an effect that you know will 'stick' (that is – you'll just leave it there without changing parameters) then you should consider making that effect a permanent change to the waveform in the Edit View later on in this book.

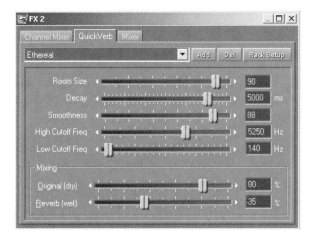

Figure 3.5
Digital effects may be applied to each track in the Multitrack View.

The most popular and useful effects are 'reverb' and 'delay'. Reverb is the ambi-ence you hear when you speak in a cathedral or gym. Delay or echo is the effect you might get as your voice bounces off a cliff and produces numerous repeating echoes.

Creating an effects rack

1 Press the 'FX' button in the track controls section to the left of the track containing the waveforms you wish to her the effect on. Drag the bar to the right of track controls towards the arrangement if you can't see the FX button.
2 The Effects Rack for that track will appear. Choose a friendly name such as 'Quick Reverb' If you like, use a 'friendly name' to describe the FX.
3 Press the + next to Delay Effects in the left hand pane and choose 'QuickVerb' from the menu.
4 Press the 'add' button to add the QuickVerb effect to the effects rack.
5 Press OK to generate the effects rack.
6 The Effects Rack dialog will close and the FX button on the Track Properties has changed to show part of the Effects Rack title. Press this button to bring up the effects rack properties for the track. This dialog has one tab for the reverb

properties and another for the effects mix for that tack. You may now play the soundtrack and choose a preset to add that reverb to the soundtrack mix.

7 Press the 'Mixer' tab to see options for balancing the dry and effected mix. These faders control the amount of signal coming back from each effect into the mix. Choose the individual effect properties to adjust the balance of wet and dry effects. You may return to the effects rack at any time by pressing the rack setup button.

Use the Rack Setup button within track effects properties to add additional effects to the effects rack.

Caution

Adobe Audition is a robust piece of software but some events are almost guaranteed to cause issues in playback. These events are almost all associated with adding effects. For best results avoid the following;

- Adding or removing effects during playback
- Numerous instances of the same effect in different tracks
- Complex effects such as long reverbs over long waveblocks

Serial and parallel effects

Effects may be applied in serial or parallel. Serial effects are chained one after the other, a little like a traditional guitarists effects pedal board. Effects used in this way are cumulative; an echo at the end of the chain will repeat the filters and chorus effects in the chain before it. Parallel effects are like effects used in a recording studio whereby each effect doesn't feed into the input of the next in the chain, the output of the effects are separate. Effects used in this way are more flexible but often aren't as creative as serial effects. Try Dynamic Eq feeding Distortion feeding Echo for a groovy example.

Figure 3.6
Effects mixer in the digital effects rack showing Parallel effects.

Tips

Edit the name of the effects in the effects rack by clicking the name of the effect in the mixers window and typing in your own.

Right click the FX button in the Track Controls for FX shortcuts

Serial and Parallel effects are mixed in different ways. Look above each of the faders in the mixers tab of any effects rack to see the Src (Source) and Pre (Previous) values for each effect. In Serial mode each effect gets 100% input from the previous

Figure 3.7

effect (effect order is decided in Rack Setup). None of the effects other than the first effect in the chain (which doesn't get these two values) receives input from the source track. Also as each effect is outputting downstream only the last fader in the chain is set above infinity. This combination of values produces the serial chain of effects with one input and one output. In parallel mode each effect is set to receive 100% of input from the source and no input from the previous effect in the chain. The number of effects in the rack determines output percentage of each fader. A rack with four effects in parallel mode will have each fader set to output at 25%. The Serial and Parallel buttons automatically calculate the settings needed to get the serial or parallel effect.

Using this system hybrid Serial/Parallel effects combinations become possible using just a percentage of the source and previous effect.

Routing track effects to alternative outputs

Track effects are bound to the host track and always appear at the output specified in the Track Properties. It's not possible to send to track effects to other tracks. However effects can be overlaid over different tracks if the effects are part of a Buss.

Limiting and managing load on the host PC when using many effects

Although native Adobe Audition effects are noticeably less hungry than VST or Direct X effects, more than three or four effects in a rack can slow down the performance of the host PC and may eventually cause it to crash. Choose View>Load Meter from the menu bar to see a visual indication of your computer's performance. Although it's not calibrated the load meter should not reach more than 20% or 30% or dropouts and skipping will occur. Echo and delay, distortion and dynamic effects use less resources than any effect intended to create a 'natural' sound. Software effects mean that we can provide a different room or ambience for every track if need be, a heaven for engineers used to working with just one or two outboard digital reverbs. Every real time effect uses more or less computer resources. Reverb is the most resource hungry effect and even two or three relatively simple reverb settings can slow down the most powerful computer. Free up these resources by mixing down tracks that are complete with effects, etc. optimised to

Info

Locking a track is possible only when an FX rack is enabled.

Tip

If your window layout gets impossible through the use of too many floating windows, the simplest way to get back to normal is to choose Settings> General (tab) and push the 'Restore Default Window Layouts' button.

that track. Select the waveblocks in the track by right clicking on any free space within the track and choosing 'Select All Blocks In Track'. Then choose Edit>Mixdown and mixdown selected waves. The mixdown will include all effects applied to the waveblocks and effects from the effects rack. The multitrack switches to Edit View with the mixdown loaded. Press Ctrl + M to load the mixdown waveblock into the multitrack view. Stereo waves may be mixed down to mono if you prefer although this doesn't free up any resources in Adobe Audition 1.0 as it will will happily render 128 stereo waveforms if you wish.

If you feel that you aren't ready to commit changes just yet you may ease the load on your PC by using the 'lock' button in the track controls. Locking a track in this way prepares effects in advance and removes the need for the program to generate effects in real time, as the session is playing. This is a very useful alternative to mixing down when wishing to preserve resources (which is all the time). Locking the track also means that the waveblock can't be moved (Lock In Time) or recorded over (Lock For Play Only) however Volume and Pan controls are enabled.

Using envelopes to create fade out and fade in effects

Dramatic fade effects can be created by drawing directly onto the waveblocks. The lines created this way are called 'envelopes'. Volume envelopes are simple to create and add dynamics to your soundtrack.

Editing volume envelopes

1 With View>Enable Envelope Editing enabled choose the volume envelope button on the main toolbar.
2 Zoom in until a light green line is visible at the top of each waveblock.
3 Press the 'Edit Envelopes' button on the toolbar to choose View>Enable Envelope Editing from the menu bar.
4 Left click on any waveblock to select, handles appear at the right and left of the light green line.

Figure 3.8
Mono Track in the multitrack view showing volume envelope and handles.

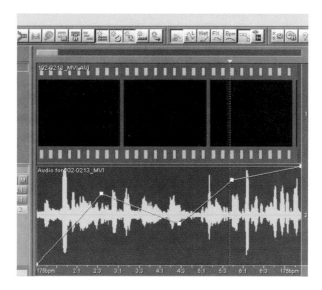

5 Move the mouse cursor over the green line, the cursor will change to a hand to indicate dragging is possible.
6 Create a diagonal line left to right across the wave by dragging the handle at the extreme right of the waveblock down towards the bottom of the block. Playback will now fade out. Create a fade in effect by reversing the line.
7 Click on the line to add more handles.
8 Drag unwanted handles off to the right or left to remove.

The session will now cause the waveblock to fade in or our depending on the position of the handles. Care must be taken as each envelope edit causes the background mix to render the session again. Pan and Wet Dry effects mix envelopes are easily edited in the same way. Drag the light blue centre line downwards to pan left, upwards to pan right. Choose 'Use Spline Envelopes' from the right click menu to even out jagged or awkward envelopes. The use of spline envelopes produces subtle effects and is often preferable, especially over vocals or other acoustic instruments.

Envelopes and automation

Automation of pan and volume is wholly achieved by the use of envelopes drawn over the waveblock. There is no automation of track mixing or muting etc. However, envelope editing is one of the ways that Adobe Audition becomes an incredibly creative tool. Drawing out a long reverb tail that crossfades with a volume envelope creates a great way to end an atmospheric track. In a studio using conventional analogue equipment this technique requires at least two people. With Audition the crossfade can be so much more complex, automatic and also saved along with the session. These envelopes have the advantage of being both easily editable and visible; the envelopes provide visual information as to the changes being made in each envelope. This is much easier than trying to remember where a fade was programmed or than trying to read the contents of a list of MIDI controller commands. The downside is that envelopes are processed in real time leading to heavy demands on system resources in a busy session. If you find that envelope changes to a particular waveblock appear to be working fine and haven't needed changing for a while, consider mixing down the waveblock to conserve system resources.

Envelopes are not applied in the Edit View. Although envelope editing has been enabled each envelope must be shown before editing is possible. To see envelopes choose View from the main menu before selecting the envelope for editing. Although it is possible to show all envelopes it's a very good idea in practise to only show one envelope at a time. Also, use the zoom vertical button on the transport bar (alternatively press alt + up arrow) until the waveblock is much larger than usual. Envelope editing is sometimes tricky and needs a larger workspace.

Additional multitrack properties

Multitrack device order

Adobe Audition will playback through as many sound cards as are installed in your computer. Output for each track can be chosen in the Track Properties. Right click over any blank space in the track controls to produce the Track Properties. Different sound cards or outputs can be arranged in order of preference. These preferences are set in Options>Device Order (F4). Under each of the four tabs is a list showing correctly installed sound cards or playback devices. By default all the devices are listed in the 'unused' column. Click the device you wish to be available first (usually the first pair of outputs 1 and 2) and add it to the device preference order by pushing the 'use' button. Do the same with the other devices in the list. It's also necessary to do this for the recording and MIDI devices but don't worry as it only has to be done once.

FX Button in Track Controls

View or change rack effects for each track. Left click to view effects. Right click to view the rack properties. This button also adopts the name given to the effects rack. Although the dialog box is called Bus Properties, these effects are not truly in a bus, as the effects rack cannot be accessed from another track. These track effects racks have more in common with 'Insert' effects that are only available to one mixer strip on a conventional mixer.

EQ Button in Track Controls

Press the EQ View button above the track controls column to see the EQ view. The EQ button within Track Controls enables presets to be created for each track. Set EQ and right click over EQ button to see EQ Presets. Press Add New and name preset. The preset will be saved along with current EQ settings for that track.

Locking a track

Lock track effects for the track. Also locks wave block position. Use the lock function for each finished track during production to increase performance. Locked tracks are rendered each time the session is loaded. Having many locked tracks in a session will noticeably slow down the loading time of a session. Locking is not enabled until effects or envelopes have been applied to that track.

View range bar

To the left of the track controls is the view range bar. Click and drag the green handle down to rapidly move between any of the 128 available tracks. Use the keyboard Alt and pointer up or down to expand or contract the number of viewable tracks in the window.

Navigator window

Press Alt + 9 to display a new window to the left of the track properties. The Navigator window has three tabs; Files, Effects and Favourites. The most useful tab is the Files tab. This is like an explorer or audio pool for the multitrack session. Audio files (although not MIDI or Video) can be dragged into this area or directly into the multitrack arrangement. Files used in the multitrack session appear in this list. Path information can also be seen.

Track Properties window

Right click over any space in the track controls area to reveal a floating Track Properties window. This window contains track controls and detailed properties for record and playback devices. As this is a floating window it may be moved outside

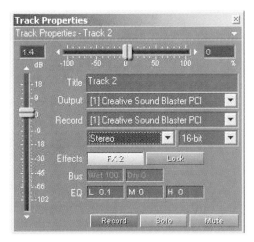

Figure 3.9
Track Properties showing options for input
and output devices.)

the main workspace to any free area on the Windows desktop. If you have a smaller monitor or are using Audition on a laptop the track properties window can be used as a 'remote control' for the program running in a much smaller window. Simply click on any track in the session to reveal track controls and properties in the Track Properties window.

Placekeeper

This is an additional window (function unknown) which may be docked anywhere alongside the other windows underneath the time display ruler. Right click the blank window to view content for the dummy window. Choose View>Show a Placekeeper to create a Placekeeper.

Tip

The transport, zoom, time window and time display controls are all contained within floating windows that may be dragged outside of the multitrack workspace. To drag a window move the cursor over the double vertical line just to the left of the button set. When the cursor changes to a double-headed arrow drag the set away. A window may be closed by clicking the X in the top right hand corner of the window. To reveal any window choose View>Show from the main view menu. Default settings can easily be recalled using the 'Restore Default Window Layouts' button on the General tab within the Options>Settings dialog.

Using Snap to make large sessions easier to handle

The display range can be several hours long if necessary – depending on the length of your waveform. Ranges longer than a few minutes can be difficult to navigate as the waveform display becomes compressed to fit into the available space inside the Adobe Audition window. Snapping helps to find the start of waveblocks or cues, etc. by forcing the playback cursor to the nearest event type selected in the Edit>Snapping menu. Most useful of these are the 'Cues', 'Blocks' and 'Loop Endpoint' options. Always use snap to Ruler and Snap To Blocks when working in Bars and Beats format as snapping will always create even length blocks which can be moved and duplicated anywhere around the session if you want to play with an arrangement.

Saving your multitrack session

To save a session choose File>Save Session. You will be prompted to save any unsaved waveblocks. If you wish to save a complete copy of a session including copies of all wave files to another location (maybe a data CD or storage device for backup) choose File>Save As and check the option to Save Copies Of All Associated Files.

Session files (*.ses)

A new session file is created when a waveblock is imported into the Multitrack. Information about waveblocks and volume, pan, EQ, effects, etc. is saved as a session file (*.ses) when the Multitrack session is saved. The multitrack session doesn't need to be a large file because it doesn't contain any audio information. The session file (usually around 10kb) simply points to any waveforms referred to in the session. Any number of sessions may refer to a single waveform and one waveform may be used any number of times in a session. A waveform file can be used in any number of sessions but changes made to the waveform itself will be carried through to all sessions in which the waveform is present. Therefore be careful when making changes to length or amplitude of a waveform if you know that it is used in another session. It is important not to move waveforms used in a Multitrack session as Audition won't be able to re-find the wave when the session is next started. If Audition can't find a waveform when loading the saved session it will prompt for the location of the file. If the session is to be exported to another computer or backed up, etc. then check the option 'Save Copies Of All Associated Files" in the Save Session dialog box. Adobe Audition will save a new copy of each waveform used in the session along with the session file in a new location.

Appending sessions

A session may be 'appended' to another session. When this happens any tracks containing waveblocks in the currently loaded session will be copied to the first free tracks in a second session and the first session will be closed. Confusingly the second session will load without the appended tracks showing; the new tracks won't be revealed until the 'display all' button is pushed. Appending sessions can be useful if for instance you have created a particular drum pattern with balances, effects, etc. just as you like them, which you wish to use in more than one session. Append to session will load your drum session into any session, importing the track properties for the drum session into the existing session. (Yes, it's confusing. Try it for yourself as it becomes clear in practice!)

1 Close all sessions.
2 Open the session containing the template tracks for importing (session A).
3 Choose File>Append To Session
4 Choose the saved session that will inherit the template tracks (session B).
5 Choose OK

Session B will open with tracks from Session A already loaded. However the tracks will be hidden. For instance if Session A contained one track, Session B will open with Track 1 out of sight. Scroll up to see the hidden track.

This first section of the book is intended to enable Adobe Audition users to quickly create and export complete movie soundtracks using pre-recorded waveforms and loops. However, Adobe Audition is able to do much more than simply play back waveforms. Many people rely on Adobe Audition because it is able to accurately record sound such as music or speech. Sound recordings can then be arranged in the multitrack to form complete compositions. The next section of the book deals with this in technical detail.

Advanced multitrack editing and recording

You've already come a long way into Adobe Audition and now have the knowledge to create stunning soundtracks. However Adobe Audition is so much more than a simple wave file arrangement tool. This chapter will introduce you to some of the deeper functions of the Adobe Audition Multitrack.

A brief introduction to 'non linear' or hard disk recording

Hard disk recording is sometimes known as 'non-linear'. This chapter starts with a brief non-technical explanation of the differences between 'linear' (start to finish) and 'non-linear' (broken pieces or sections of music) recording.

Imagine making a tape recording. A large reel of magnetic tape is loaded onto a tape recorder. The recording starts, the tape is pulled across a magnetic head and taken up onto an empty reel. Then the music starts and is recorded onto the tape. The tape recorder records whatever microphones etc. pick up and the sound is then 'stuck' permanently in one position on that reel of tape. In many ways the tape is the music from then on. The performance is over and the musicians may go home, the only record is that single piece of tape. During the recording the performance is permanently encoded onto the tape and can only be moved forwards or backwards in time in one way; a section of the tape must be cut out and replaced with another section taken from elsewhere in the recording. This process is destructive because the tape is permanently changed. In fact before editing a safety copy is always made in case of accidents. If the edit doesn't work for some reason then the tape can't be melded back together again. The original performance has been changed forever. This is linear recording; the performance starts in one place on the tape and ends in another. Until the tape is physically changed forever, the performance is set almost in stone.

Imagine you wanted to record a band or even an orchestra but you wanted a separate recording of each performer, so you could go back later and adjust the balance or even mute parts of the recording. You'd need a tape recorder placed in front of each musician. This is no problem. But what happens when you want to start recording? You must run round the room starting each tape recorder, one at a time. So you think "OK... I'll ask the musicians to do it" And being an obliging bunch they do. But when you want to play back, it's impossible to start all the tapes playing at the same time. Even if you managed to get two going exactly at the same time the varying motor speed of each tape recorder would mean that no two tape players could ever play exactly in time from beginning to end, even for

29

more than a few seconds. To get around this you build a new invention – a new tape recorder that has four little tape recorders all stacked on top of each other. And here's the good bit; they all use the same tape. So the recording and playback stays exactly in time because the tape sticks all of the performances together at the same time. They are synchronised because the tape holds them in one place. The multitrack recording is linear also; it starts at the beginning and ends at the end. The performances are stuck to the tape.

Imagine in your dreams that you were able to slice the multitrack tape lengthways into much thinner strips and cut sections from each performance or 'track'. So for a chorus section of your song you'd have four (or more) little pieces of tape; one each from the bass player, guitarist, keyboards and drums. Now imagine that you could keep these small pieces perfectly preserved and intact but at the same time clone and reproduce them at any time. The situation has now changed. The performances are now valuable material, which can be used and reused forever, in a hundred different recordings. Any new song or musical production made from these performances no longer contains the memory of four or so people playing at the same time but the reproduction of many different performances, some repeated over and over again. And if the new record doesn't work, the performances can be reused. Each performance is like paint in a never-ending tube to be applied to a digital canvas wherever the producer feels like it. This is non-linear recording; individual performances taken from anywhere in a recording, maybe even from a different song or session and moved or swapped backwards and forwards in time. The recording no longer starts with 1-2-3-4. It can now begin at the end and work backwards.

An Adobe Audition multitrack arrangement is non-linear because it is composed of as many wave blocks as you like. The wave blocks may be moved backwards or forwards in time and wave blocks containing recordings from different sessions can be used. The important thing to remember in the Multitrack View is that any changes to the sound of the wave such as dynamic effects or even volume envelopes are 'non-destructive'; the original performance waveform is unchanged.

Recording directly into a multitrack session – multitrack recording

Multitrack recording in the Multitrack View enables the user to record a brand new waveform while listening to other waveforms, as if using a multitrack tape machine (Figure 4.1). Adobe Audition enables the creation of multiple waves in a multitrack session very, very simple. However the eventual success of the session relies on a few simple things all working at the same time. This is a checklist to use until working in this view becomes second nature. Then you'll wonder what all the fuss was about.

- Check the track properties to make sure that the primary input and output devices are set to be the first pair of devices (usually 1 and 2) of your sound card. Push the Out1 button in the track controls bar and check the box marked 'same for all tracks' to clone this setting. Do the same with the Rec1 button.
- Check your Device Properties for the Record Device (Rec1). The devices and configuration settings shown here will depend on the sound card installed in the host computer. Default settings for sample rate and bit depth are set in Options>Settings>Multitrack. If you choose stereo input in this dialog but later

Figure 4.1
A complete multitrack session showing numerous waveblocks and loops.

on choose to create a new mono waveform both sides of the assigned stereo input will be summed in the new mono waveform. This is the recommended method as no stereo information is lost of recording in mono. Be critical when choosing which parts to record in stereo. Remember that a stereo waveblock requires twice as many resources as a mono waveblock. On the other hand a powerful system should have no problems manipulating stereo wave blocks of a reasonable length and the results will be better than mono.

- Right click over the display time ruler just below the track window and choose the appropriate display time for your recording. Usually this will be decimal; Minutes, Seconds, Decimal (MM:SS:DDD) or Bars and Beats depending on your plans for the session. Decimal time is rounded to 3 places in the large time display. Each second is divided into 999 frames. If you plan to work in Beats Per Minute (BPM) choose Bars and Beats from the display time format menu. Right click again over the large time display and choose Edit Tempo. Enter the desired BPM in Edit Tempo properties. Remember to enable the metronome (Options>Metronome) if you desire.

Congratulations! Your multitrack session is now set up.

With your sound source properly connected to the computer, press F10 to enable the level display meters. The meters will move in time with the levels received from the sound card.

Recording the first track

Right click over any grey area in the track controls bar to see a floating 'Track Properties' window (Figure 4.2). Set the controls here to reflect your preferences. The default settings in this illustration are a good place to start. Keep the floating track properties window open and simply click on any other track to see properties for that track. Choose Track 1 and press the red button 'R' to arm the track. More than one track may be armed at any time but tracks cannot be armed while playing or recording. 'Rec1' button to confirm the track is assigned to that device. Use Ctrl + Spacebar to start recording, spacebar to stop

Figure 4.2
Track Properties for Track One in the Multitrack View

Tip

Adobe Audition will record for as long as you keep playing. A wave block is created in each track set to record ready whenever recording is started. A session is always easier to manage if the display range is set to roughly the length of the song before recording actually begins. However, Adobe Audition is set by default to simply display a range of 30 seconds whenever a new Multitrack session is loaded. To lengthen the ranges create a short empty wave block of around 10 seconds in any track. Then duplicate this block as many times as necessary to force the display range to the length of your song. Delete the empty wave blocks when the display range is as long as required.

To make the new waveform 'safe' right click over the fresh waveform. Choose 'Lock In Time' and 'Lock For Play Only' from the menu (Figure 4.3). These options will ensure that the new recording cannot be overwritten, no matter what other settings are applied elsewhere in the session. Test this by re-arming the same track. The locked waveform will remain green with a small icon indicating the locked status of the waveblock in the lower right hand corner of the waveblock.

Recording additional tracks is a simple as 'arming' further tracks and creating wave blocks to size as before. If each wave block is locked in time Adobe Audition will never lose the arrangement, each wave block will behave just as a tape track – with some notable additional features.

Figure 4.3
A newly recorded waveblock with Lock In Time and Lock for Play only set. Note that the Track is still record enabled. Further waveforms may be recorded into this track but this waveform cannot now be overwritten.

Here are some rules for 'best practice' in the multitrack view.

- Always lock wave blocks in time as soon as they are created.
- Write disable new wave blocks after a successful 'take' by choosing 'Lock for Play Only' from the wave block properties menu.
- Disarm all tracks before arming a fresh track for recording.
- Use Zoom Out buttons to reveal additional free tracks (up to a total of 128).
- Save often.

Saving the new session and waveblocks
It's impossible to save a session without saving, or choosing not to save, all associated waveblocks used in the session.

The Mix Gauge and background mixing

If you want to jump right in and record, go ahead. Adobe Audition is a tough and intuitive piece of software and you'll have no trouble figuring it out. But take five minutes to read this section and see what a great piece of software you just bought.

Below the track properties bar is the Mix Gauge (Figure 4.4). This gauge reads from left to right. When the gauge is full Adobe Audition is ready to roll and will perform flawlessly producing effects and EQ with no problem. Playback may happen if the gauge is less than half full but effects and EQ values may not seem to happen and playback may skip. This isn't a fault. Other audio software appears to play back immediately. But the results are inferior. This is because to produce all those cool rack effects and EQ etc in real time it's necessary to cut some corners and reduce the amount of information the computer processor is asked to handle. This is achieved by simply dropping some information, some sounds in other words. It sounds OK but A/B the result with Adobe Audition and you'll see what's missing. Adobe Audition works in a different way rendering each mix before playing

Figure 4.4
Mix gauge showing mix completed. Right Click over the mix gauge to see mixing options.

back. Each edit or adjustment in the Multitrack view (although not in the edit view) causes the program to re-render (or mix) the session again and so sends the mix gauge back to zero for a short time while the new audio picture is built. This process enables Adobe Audition to preserve the quality of the recorded waveforms and effects, etc. treats your work with respect and produces a brilliant finish in very little time. If problems appear when playing back a complex mix with lots of effects, EQ and envelope, just check and see how the Mix Gauge is, sit back and wait for a few seconds if necessary and try again.

Right click over the mix gauge to see options for background mixing. In some situations it may be desirable to disable background mixing completely. This may be useful if you need to make several envelope changes or effects changes to your mix and want to delay the background mix until all the edits are completed. Depending on the system resources of the host computer it may also be beneficial to choose whether or not to mix the whole session or a shorter period of time; 10 or 20 seconds ahead from this menu. Additional options for prioritising the background mix are also available from this menu. The Mix Priority options attempt to remove some of the guesswork necessary to configure Adobe Audition correctly. Choose whether to enable Adobe Audition to prioritise background mixing ahead of other tasks or not. The most appropriate setting for this will depend on your system and the number of waveforms, busses and effects used n the current session. Some experimentation is necessary to produce the optimum settings. Start by choosing the super high priority and experiment with lower priorities until the trade off between playback and performance becomes acceptable to you.

Recording a new multitrack session using bars and beats

Instant gratification: recording to a click

1 Start Adobe Audition.
2 Switch to Multitrack View.
3 Ensure time window is showing time in bars and beats.
4 Set Tempo and time signature in Options>Metronome.
5 Enable the Metronome.
6 Arm a track and record.

Simple as that!

Hint

Right click over the large time display and choose 'Bars and Beats' when creating musical arrangements. If you want that comfortable 'snap to bar' feeling, use Bars and Beats display (right click over the time display window) and choose Snapping to Ruler (coarse). The playback cursor will land at the beginning of the nearest bar.

Snapping

Adobe soundtracks are created using waveblocks related to waveforms created and recorded earlier in the session or during a completely different session. A waveblock may contain just a single drum hit or an entire guitar solo. The waveblocks need to be arranged inside the Multitrack View, one after the other, or playing at the same time to create a song. This is much easier if the waveblocks are a set length, usually a bar or an equal division of a bar.

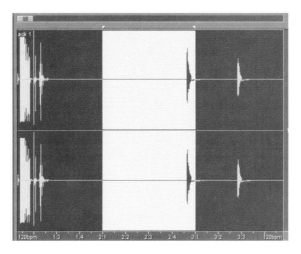

Figure 4.5
A range of one bar length (bar two) has been selected over this waveform. Snapping to Ruler (Coarse) enables simple accurate range selections.

To create musically useful waveblocks inside the multitrack view we have to use the 'snap to' feature like this;

1   Record your part along with the metronome (as laid out above).
2   Choose Edit>Snapping>Snap to Ruler (Coarse).
3   Click inside the new waveblock as close as possible to the start of the downbeat.
4   Click and drag along the waveblock for as many bars or beats as necessary.
5   Right click inside the selected range and choose Trim from the drop down menu.
6   Right click and drag to move the resized waveblock anywhere within the multitrack view.

Right click over the new part and choose Waveblock properties to rename the part. The right click menu also contains options for changing the colour of the waveblock and for duplicating and looping the part. As long as the Snapping function remains set to bars and beats the new part can easily be moved with the multitrack view and will snap to the nearest bar so always remaining in time with the song. Many people have found that creating and moving parts like this is easier than with other software as Adobe Audition doesn't need to rely on the first note in the part appearing exactly on the downbeat. If necessary, the fine resolution enables the user to create parts that don't happen to start exactly on the first beat of the bar. This is especially important when recording string parts or anything that has a slow attack.

Creating loops and duplicating wave blocks

After creating, trimming and moving the new part the second most important technique to get hold of in Adobe Audition is the duplication (looping) function. Adobe Audition doesn't have a 'pencil tool' however looping any part is simple and powerful – if not immediately obvious!

Figure 4.6
Four beats in this waveform have been selected and loop properties have been set to enable this waveform to loop correctly.

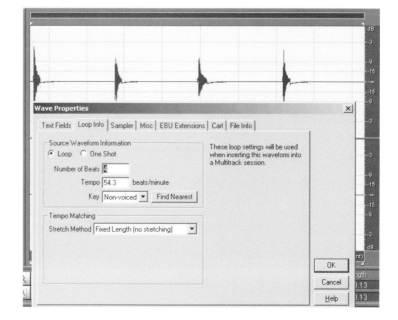

1 Record a new part along with your session in the multitrack view.
2 Double click the new waveblock to load the waveblock in edit view.
3 Find the start and end of the section to be looped (much easier if you have Snap to Bars and Beats enabled), If necessary preview the loop in the edit view and adjust start and end points until it feels right.
4 Select this area, right click over the selected area and choose Trim from the menu.
5 Choose View>Wave Properties>Loop Info (Figure 4,7).
6 Select 'Enable Looping' and ensure that the correct number of beats in the loop is set (Adobe Audition will work out the tempo).
7 Save the new waveform, ensuring that the box 'Save any extra non-audio information' is checked.
8 Press F12 to return to the multitrack view.
9 Disarm the track and select the wave then right click to select 'Loop Properties' from the drop down menu.
10 Check 'Enable Looping' and choose the option to repeat after so many beats (the same number of beats as your waveform).
11 Ensure that 'Time Scale Stretch' is selected if you want your loop to follow the session tempo.

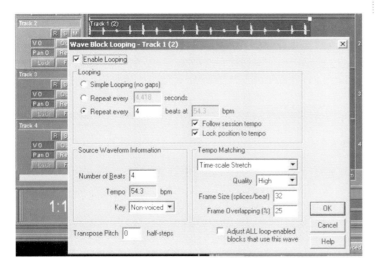

Figure 4.7
The saved waveform is loaded into the Multitrack View and set to loop in time with the session.

The waveblock will appear with a new icon, indicating that loop properties are enabled. At the same time 'Block Edge Dragging' has been enabled, indicated by three lines at the right edge of the waveblock. Dragging over this edge will cause the waveblock to grow by any amount, causing the contents to be repeated by whole bars, half bars or any amount. A repeated section may be duplicated or a unique copy can be made of any looped section in the usual way.

Translating loop values to musical notation

The 'repeat every' value doesn't easily translate if you are the kind of person who is used to counting four in a bar. Enter the following values in the 'Repeat every' field within the Wave Block Looping dialog in Loop Properties.

Repeat every

.25	creates	Semiquavers (sixteenth notes)
.50	creates	Quavers (eighth notes)
1	creates	Crotchet note (quarter note)
2	creates	Minims (half notes)
4	creates	Semibreve (whole note)

Fractions or odd numbers may also be used to create other intervals.

Time stretching and changing session tempo

Adobe Audition offers 'recycle' like features enabling the playback properties of looped waveblocks to follow the session tempo. This is not enabled by default. To enable this feature choose the option 'Time Scale Stretch' from the Tempo Matching tools within the Loop Properties for each looped waveform. Also ensure that 'Follow Session Tempo' is also checked. Now if the session tempo is changed (View>Advanced Session Properties or Ctrl-I) all looped waveforms set like this will automatically be time stretched to fit the new tempo. If you have created copies of a looped section (Shift – Right click and drag) the option 'Adjust ALL loop-enabled blocks that use this wave' must be checked for the entire session to follow the tempo changes. Incidentally, while this powerful feature is great for adjustments of a few beats or more – extreme changes can cause unwanted side effects such as artifacts and timing errors.

Choose the Resample option from Tempo Matching tools to change the pitch as well as the tempo when following session tempo. Waveblocks containing loops and beats require 'Beat Splice' from the Tempo Matching options

Simple duplication

If the session contains cues or layers that wouldn't benefit from time stretching etc. these can be duplicated simply by right clicking over the waveblock and choosing 'Loop Duplicate' from the menu.

Waveforms containing loop information can be reused in other Adobe Audition sessions (although not in any other program) as the loop information enables the waveblock to adapt itself to any new session tempo etc. Looped waveforms can also be saved in the Adobe Audition *.cel format. Most importantly, the looping information which enables the waveblock to be reused at a different tempo or pitch is applied only when the waveblock is used in a multitrack session therefore it is non-destructive; the waveblock remains just as it was recorded.

Hint

Group Normalizing waveforms can save time and produce a much better result for your session. Waveforms that have been recorded at different times from different sessions or studios often differ in levels. This makes it difficult to mix the session as balancing has to be done to compensate for the different waveforms before the real mixing can go ahead. Use the Group Normalise function (Edit>Group Normalise) to normalise each of the waveforms in the session to the same amount.

Adobe Audition as a virtual recording studio

Creating a brand new composition

Follow these steps to create a brand new composition using pre-recorded loops along with instruments recorded directly into the program. For this step through I used CELs distributed with the upgrade available to registered Cool Edit Pro owners by Adobe.

Create a rhythm track using a pre-recorded CEL

- Drag SlickFunkDrm01.cel onto track one and drag back to the beginning of the arrangement.
- Drag the shaded area of the waveform along the track to paint seven more loops.
- Press play to hear the drum part loop seamlessly.

Figure 5.1
A loaded CEL is playing as a loop.

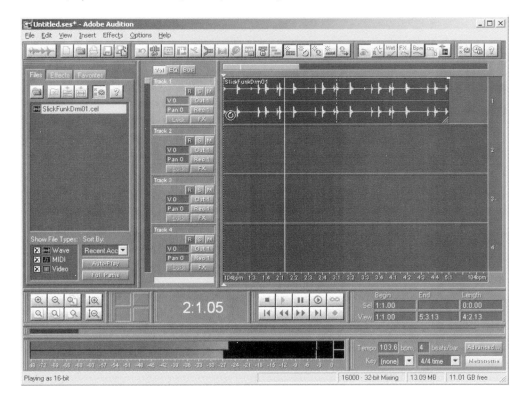

Add dynamics processing to the drum part.

Dynamics processing lowers the dynamic range of the waveform. In this way the difference between quiet parts and loudest parts is reduced without raising the overall level of the waveform to avoid clipping.

- Stop the playback
- Choose the effects tab and find Dynamics Processing in the Real Time Effects group.
- Drag the dynamics processing effect on top of the rhythm track. It doesn't matter if you drag it on top of the waveblock.
- From the drop down menu in the effect properties choose the Drum Machine Limiter preset
- Start playback. The rhythm part is now more exciting to listen to.

Working through the multitrack session towards a finished song

We can use this rhythm part as the seed for a brand new multitrack session that will eventually become your soundtrack

Other instrumental recordings

Prepare your bass part and record it and additional rhythm parts on tracks two, three and four.

1 Arm track two by pressing the record button in the track controls. Ensure that only Track One is armed.
2 Press F10 to preview record levels, F10 again when OK.
3 Press play to rehearse the new part as many times as you wish. When ready use Ctrl + Spacebar to start recording, spacebar when finished.
4 Right click over the new part and Lock In Time.
5 Save session and waveforms.
6 If necessary double click on either the bass waveblock or the file in the navigator to load the waveblock in edit view and make any adjustments to amplitude or envelope etc. The new waveform can be truncated (trimmed of any empty space at the beginning and end) to save space.

Recording and choosing different 'takes'

When the Multiple Takes option is enabled each new pass doesn't simply replace the content of the waveblock. Each 'take' creates a brand new waveblock, which may be reviewed after recording is completed. In this way numerous attempts can be made at a difficult passage without losing any previous recordings.

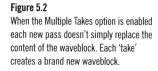

Figure 5.2
When the Multiple Takes option is enabled each new pass doesn't simply replace the content of the waveblock. Each 'take' creates a brand new waveblock.

1 Disarm all tracks and record enable track three.
2 Record your first attempt.
3 After recording right click over the new waveblock and choose 'Allow Multiple Takes'.
4 Re-record as many attempts as you wish.
5 Right click over the new waveblock and choose 'Take History' to select a list of previous takes. Select any take to load into the waveblock.

Punching in

'Punching in' is the name given to the technique of correcting errors made during the recording by setting the recorder to record over the poor section of the performance. This technique is typically used when a near perfect take has a minor mistake somewhere which needs to be erased but without recording over the rest of the take. It's called 'Punching In' because the engineer first starts the tape rolling and then jabs at the record button moments before the mistake, then again moments after to stop recording and preserve the remainder. This is very difficult to do right and can easily result in more mistakes. Adobe Audition automates this procedure and makes it easy to undo any errors.

1 Disarm all tracks and record enable track four.
2 Record a simple solo or vocal for a few bars.
3 Find a poorly performed section of the waveblock then click and drag to select an area just before and after the 'mistake' (Figure 5.3). Choose this area carefully; ideally it should begin and end in an area of silence after a word or phrase. Punching in mid-section is difficult as the performer is rarely able to sing or play the same thing twice!
4 Right click over this area and choose 'Punch In' from the menu. The waveform will splice itself into three areas and the track will arm (if not already armed). The selected area will become red to indicate it's recordable status while the remainder of the track will stay green to indicate that these areas will not be recorded over.
5 Place the playback cursor at a suitable point before the punch in and press Ctrl+Spacebar to start recording.
6 After recording review each take by choosing and loading each from the Take History menu and choose the best one. With the best take loaded choose 'Merge This Take' from the Take History menu. The currently loaded take will be permanently merged into the waveblock.

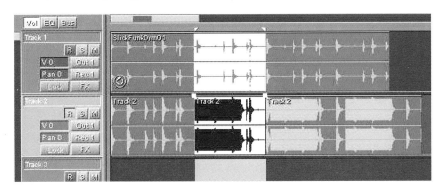

Figure 5.3
A newly recorded waveform has been enabled for punching in.

Using a stereo input pair as two mono inputs

Sometimes every hermit engineer and producer has so get outside and face the real world of microphones and musicians. A common task is to create a stereo recording but have each a separate mono waveform for each of the microphones (channel splitting)

1 In multitrack view click the record selection button (Rec1) in the Track Controls for track one.
2 In the Record Devices dialog ensure that the Track will receive information from the left channel only (choose 32bit recording of course).
3 Click the record selection button for Track 2.
4 In the Record Devices dialog ensure Track 2 will receive information from the right channel only.

Both channels will now record information coming from only the left and right channels of the sound card input. This obviously depends on the microphones being routed correctly.

Managing a session

Just like any conventional recording session your Adobe Audition session can quickly become cluttered with junk. Empty waveforms, muted waveforms, waveforms behind each other and overlong waveforms are just a few of the things that can make a simple session seem much more complicated than it should be. And remember that even empty and muted waveforms are making a hit on your processor time. So kick out the junk from time to time like this.

Deadheading your waveforms

A 'waveform' is the original recording. A 'waveblock' is an image of that recording in the multitrack view. Waveblocks can be edited and deleted from the multitrack view without affecting the source waveform.

Truncating (or deadheading) waveforms used in the session before saving can save storage space. A waveform that contains nothing more than empty space or silence still contains data; the data is simply a long row of nothing! All this silence takes expensive storage space so trim the silence from the beginning and end of each waveform before saving.

Double click on each waveform to load the waveform in Edit View. Select the silence or unwanted noise at the beginning and end of the waveform by clicking and dragging across the areas of no data – 'flat lines'. It's important to remember that very quiet sounds may not be seen at some resolutions so audition the waveform before deleting vital sounds. If your session contains a waveblock with occasional events such as a cymbals track it's a good idea to remove the empty space as this will remove load from the computer so freeing up room for more exciting things like effects. Deleting areas at the beginning and end of a waveform while in the Edit View won't cause the associated waveblock to change position. However, if a range is removed from the middle of a waveform the waveblock will shrink around the deleted area and events will move out of time in the session. Always right click over a brand new recorded waveblock and choose Lock In Time from the right click menu before editing waveforms. When the unwanted areas are identified drag-select and press the delete key to remove the silence or noise.

Trimming and deleting waveblocks

The session can become very confusing if waveblocks have excess space before and after the content. 'Deadhead' waveblocks by clicking and dragging over silence in the waveblock and pressing the delete key to remove the selected area. It doesn't matter if you accidentally remove content while deleting, as the source waveform is not affected. When you are sure that these edits will work double click to load the waveblock into edit view and remove the space permanently but remember to lock in time before doing so. Again, it helps if Snap to Ruler is enabled as fixed length waveblocks will be created which can be easily be moved around the session. Either choose 'Full' from the right click menu to return the waveblock to it's previous unedited state (if you haven't edited the waveform by now) or enable 'Block Edge Dragging' (Block Edge Dragging button on the main toolbar) and drag the extreme left or right edge of the waveblock over the recently created space. Remove a complete waveblock by selecting and pressing the delete key on the keyboard or by choosing 'Remove' from the right click menu.

Permanently destroy a waveblock and close the source waveform by selecting the waveblock and choosing 'Destroy' from the right click menu. This action will remove the waveblock and close but not delete the source waveform. Selecting this option prompts Adobe Audition to ask if you wish to close the file as it is being used by the multitrack session. Answering no removes just that waveblock. Answering Yes removes the waveblock and all waveblocks referencing the source waveform. For instance all split sections of a waveblock will be removed.

Splitting, merging and grouping waveblocks

Sometimes a waveblock needs to be split into sections. To split a single waveblock place the playback cursor anywhere over a waveblock, right click and choose 'Split' from the menu to split the waveblock in two. To rejoin two split sections select just one half (or section) and choose 'Merge' from the right click menu. It's not possible to merge two sections from different waveblocks. Sometimes it's useful to group waveblocks together. Grouped waveblocks can be moved or removed as one. Ctrl + left click over two or more waveblocks and choose 'Group' from the right click menu to group waveblocks. The colour of a group can be useful for instance when identifying which waveblocks contain drums or percussion in a busy session. Choose 'group colour' from the right click menu to change the colour of a group. Alternatively, to change the colour of just one waveblock that may not be part of a

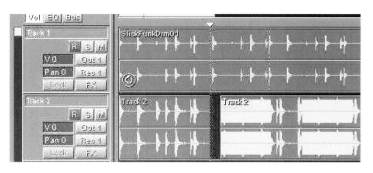

Figure 5.4
A waveform has been split and the right section has been moved away from the left.

group; right click over the waveblock and choose Waveblock Properties from the menu. Waveblock properties in this dialog are duplicated elsewhere but the Hue slider is useful for identifying waveblocks by colour. Simply move the slider right or left to change the colour of the waveblock.

Selecting multiple waveblocks

Move or delete more than one waveblock by clicking on the first then holding the Ctrl key and clicking on further waveblocks. All selected waveblocks can then be moved or deleted as one.

Inserting and deleting time in a session

Sometimes it may be useful to insert extra bars into a session (global insert). Place the playback cursor at the point where the insert is to be made and right click over any empty space in a track. The whole track doesn't need to be empty but the Insert Time option isn't available in the waveblock properties right click menu. Choose Insert Time from the right click menu and the amount of time to be inserted (Figure 5.5). Waveblocks to the right of the cursor are moved to the right. Delete time (global cut) by selecting a range using the mouse and right clicking over any empty space. The Delete Selected Time option is now enabled.

Figure 5.5
Two bars are just about to be inserted into the session at bar two. All blocks in the session will be split and the right hand side of the split will be moved ahead by two bars.

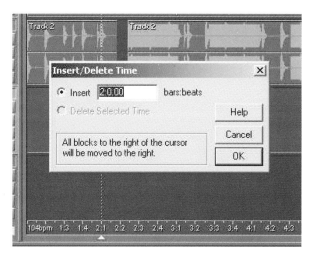

Default session

Any session may be saved as the default session. Once a default session has been created each subsequent session will inherit track properties, EQ and effects settings, busses, etc. from the default setting. Using default settings can save a considerable amount of time, particularly if new sessions generally contain the same effects configurations etc. Waveblocks may be saved in the default session although Adobe Audition will prompt you to confirm that the waveblocks may not be there in future sessions. The default session will only load on the File>New Session command. Sessions with their own track properties are not overwritten by the default session.

Clearing space in temp files

Adobe Audition is pretty good about clearing up around itself (just like any good assistant) but if your system is low on storage space you may find a slight performance benefit from periodically removing any unused temporary files using this dialog. Each open waveform is displayed with five levels of undo history. Delete the no longer needed undo history to shrink the temporary files. Currently open files may also be closed in this way although the currently loaded file in the Edit View may not be closed.

Advanced recording in the multitrack session

When preparing to record a complex session, particularly one with many small waveblocks, it's a good idea to create, name and save one empty track length waveform for each track you plan to use. During the recording use block split, lock in time and lock for play only to manipulate and arrange the numerous waveblocks. However many splits and edits are eventually created, the session will still only have as many waveforms as were created before the recording started.

This technique avoids the numerous small files that are created for each missed cue or fluffed line and makes managing the session waveforms much easier. Additionally as each waveform usually contains only one instrument or part (one for bass, one for guitar, etc.) it's much easier to apply effects and filters to the whole track without mixing down several small waveforms etc.

Mixing down

A complete Adobe Audition session could contain hundreds of waveblocks, volume and pan envelopes, etc. Adobe Audition is able to manipulate the session very well but the program will work faster and your session quality will improve if you are able to mix down periodically as you work. This is a good way to improve performance of your system, particularly if your session uses a large number of effects and envelope changes.

A completed part that contains many associated waveblocks, such as a string or horn arrangement may be mixed down to one full-length stereo waveblock containing effects and envelope changes etc in the mixed waveform. The mixdown waveblock can then be incorporated into a brand new post-production session consisting of one song-length waveform for drums, one for horns, one for bass etc. Resource hungry mastering effects can then be applied to the post-production session leaving the original session intact.

It's not unusual for clients to insist on four or five alternative arrangements and mixes. Getting used to the idea that a song may have more than one finished version is just part of the job of a successful record or soundtrack production team.

1 Left click on a waveblock to select.
2 Hold the ctrl key and left click on another waveblock to group waveblocks.
3 Right click over any waveblock in the group and choose Mix Down from the menu. Choose mono or stereo mixdown depending on the content. Space can be saved if you mixdown a group of stereo waves to a mono wave or pan and volume envelopes can be created for multiple mono waves, which can then be mixed down into one stereo wave.

The mixdown will appear in the track navigator if it is open. If not, choose Insert>File/Cue List from the menu bar and choose the new mixdown from this list. The mixdown feature may be used when creating a stereo master mixdown of a completed session but it can only contain the contents of waveblocks in Adobe Audition and not information from external devices such as MIDI modules, etc. To include sounds from external tone modules, samplers, etc. It's necessary to route the output from the computer sound card through an external mixer along with the output from external modules and record the result to DAT or Mini Disk etc. in the 'traditional' way. Another solution is to route the output of the tone module into the sound card and use Adobe Audition to record the tone module as if it were a 'live' performance.

Busses

Figure 5.6

To an audio engineer a bus is like a one-way street with many entrances but only one end – the output. Each waveform joining the bus is merged with any the other waveforms and accepts EQ and effects assigned to the bus. Busses are useful when one effects rack can be used over two or more tracks. The effects rack may contain a favourite reverb and delay combination that is suitable for backing vocals and a string pad. Instead of creating a separate and resource hungry effects rack for each track create a new effects bus and route each track through that bus.

Left clicking on the Playback device button in the track controls produces the Playback Devices dialog box. In the lower pane of this dialog is a window showing busses already created either in this session or as part of the default session if one has been saved. To create a new bus choose New Bus in the dialog and give the bus a 'Friendly Name' that will show on the track controls button. Select the appropriate effects and output device for the bus and press OK to save. The bus is now available as a new output device. Right click on the new button in the track controls to jump to the effects properties for that bus.

Crossfading, and other advanced envelope techniques

Crossfading is the technique of fading one track out while fading another in. Enable the volume envelope and draw a fade curve out over the first waveblock and a curve in on the second. To automatically create a fade in or out select a section at the beginning or end of the song and right click over the selected area. Choose 'crossfade' from the menu and your choice of crossfade 'flavour' depending on the track and your own tastes. To clear a whole bunch of incorrect volume or pan-handles (no joke intended!) select an area of the waveform and choose Clear Envelope from the menu.

Figure 5.7
This section of a waveform has been crossfaded.

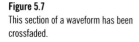

Wet and dry envelopes

The FX button on each track control acts like an insert effect for that track only. The track is routed through the effects rack before the track controls take effect. The Wet/Dry envelope controls the wet/dry (effects balance) mix of the effects rack for each track. It does not enable real time control of the effects bus. Dragging the handle to the top of the waveblock causes the effect to be applied at 100%. Draw envelopes over waveblocks to create crossfading of effects during the session.

FX parameter envelopes

Some effects such as the Dynamic EQ effect have parameters that may be drawn directly onto the waveblock as envelopes. Each property that may be edited with an envelope in real time is identified within the effect properties within the effects rack for each track. Different effects have different properties; for example the dynamic EQ effect uses pink and yellow envelopes to describe the movement of the eq and gain curve. Envelopes are not copied when waveblocks are duplicated.

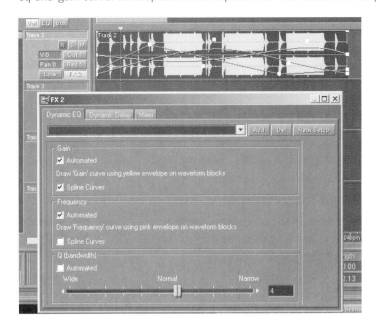

Figure 5.8
Dynamic Delay and Dynamic EQ envelopes drawn on a waveblock.

Tempo envelopes

Tempo envelopes are display-only envelopes for MIDI files. If a MIDI file is inserted into the session and the envelope feature is enabled you'll see a red line with numbers showing the tempo at each spot in the MIDI file. A MIDI file with no tempo changes will just show a flat line with a number at the front of the file. Right click over the MIDI file and choose Tempo from the menu to edit the playback tempo in BPM. Alternatively the tempo may be set to match the session tempo.

MIDI and SMTPE/MTC

Adobe Audition works with the operating system to enable MIDI file playback (not creating or editing) of MIDI files from within the Multitrack View. Adobe Audition is also able to react to triggers produced by a sequencer or any other MIDI equipment and transmitted to the computer over MIDI. Additionally, Adobe Audition is able to act as a master or a slave device in a SMPTE/MTC sync situation.

MIDI data enters the PC through a MIDI interface. This may be an external device featuring numerous MIDI input and output connections such as a USB Midisport or similar. Alternatively the PC may have a MIDI socket as a feature of the internal soundcard.

MIDI/ SMPTE sync is only possible in the Multitrack View.

Tip

If you can't seem to get MIDI to work at all check the connections where your MIDI cables meet your computer and where the MIDI cable meets your equipment. MIDI sockets are one-way either in or out of the device. For MIDI information to get into the computer it's necessary for the MIDI out of your equipment to meet the MIDI input of your computer and vice-versa. Two MIDI cables are usual, one for MIDI in and one for MIDI out. Connect the MIDI output of your controller keyboard or device to the MIDI in of the computer sound card. Connect the MIDI out of the computer sound card to the MIDI in of any tone module.

Because MIDI cables do not carry audio data it is impossible to record the sound of any MIDI keyboard even when the MIDI cables are connected. MIDI only enables the software inside the keyboard to talk to software inside another keyboard or computer etc. Audio cables must be connected to hear the sound of the equipment. Windows 95 has a limit of 11 MIDI devices. Upgrade to Windows 98 before attempting to use a multiport sound card in your computer.

MIDI file formats

Adobe Audition provides MIDI functionality limited to playback of MIDI files (Type 0 and 1). Type O MIDI files contain data in just one track. Type 1 MIDI files contain data in any number of tracks. Both types of MIDI file transmit data on 16 channels. Adobe Audition is able to decode and pass data from the MIDI file to any internal or external MIDI device.

Opening and controlling playback properties of a MIDI file

Within the Multitrack View start a new session and choose Insert>MIDI From File from the menu bar. Browse and select any MIDI file. The MIDI file is automatically inserted in the first free track. Alternatively use the Navigator (Alt + 9) and drag a currently loaded MIDI file from the Navigator to anywhere within the session. MIDI blocks are similar to waveblocks in that they may be split and duplicated etc. but MIDI blocks do not have loop properties.

Playback properties for the MIDI file may be adjusted using the right click menu. The entire MIDI block may be transposed using 'Transpose' or MIDI Tempo may be changed using 'Set Tempo' In this way the overall playback speed of the MIDI file may be changed to suit the tempo of the track. Tempo information contained in the MIDI file may be seen by choosing View>Show Tempo Envelopes from the title bar or by choosing the appropriate button from the Menu Bar.

MIDI mapping

Mapping instruments to MIDI channels enables the user to control which device or port a particular instrument will be sent to. MIDI devices (internal and external) have 16 channels each. Some MIDI controllers or interfaces have more than one MIDI output port. Additionally your system soundcard probably has a GM (General MIDI) synthesiser built in. Use the MIDI mapping feature to control which instruments are sent to which port.

For instance you may have a dedicated MIDI drum module on Port A and a General MIDI synth (with less dramatic drum sounds) on Port B. In this case the drum parts from the MIDI file (usually on Channel 10) would be mapped to Port A while all the other instruments are mapped to Port B. See MIDI Mapping options by pressing the MAP button within the track controls bar in the multitrack view (the map button is only present for MIDI tracks). Choose an instrument from the top of the dialog and choose a Device and channel to map to from the lower two boxes. Channels without alternative mapping are simply transmitted on their default channel. Shift-click to select more than one instrument. If you wish to re-map an entire MIDI file to another port it is necessary to select the whole 16 channels.

Active tracks

If necessary just one channel may be selected for playback using the active tracks feature (right click menu over any MIDI track in the Multitrack View). The active track data is highlighted within the MIDI track.

Controller 7 value

MIDI Controller 7 is the Volume controller for each MIDI channel.

Volume envelopes over a MIDI block

Adobe Audition enables drawing of volume envelopes over a MIDI block in the same way as envelopes may be drawn over a waveblock. This is a convenient way of creating fades, etc.

SMPTE / MTC synchronisation

Adobe Audition is able to send and receive MTC (SMPTE over MTC) information using MIDI ports. SMPTE (audio) information is converted to MIDI data by the program before being sent to another program or transmitted outside the computer. SMPTE must be converted to MIDI by an external device if the PC is to be used as a SMPTE slave. Adobe Audition is also able to act as a master device enabling synchronisation and control of external devices to the host computer. Enable Options>SMPTE Slave Enable to force the program to wait for a valid SMPTE offset before starting playback. While in playback mode the internal clock is synchronised to the frequency of the SMPTE code arriving via MIDI. In this way Adobe Audition is able to closely follow tape based recordings or video.

To enable Adobe Audition as a master device

Select Options>SMPTE Master to transmit SMPTE code during playback and so sync with tape or video. SMPTE code display is shown in master and slave mode.

To enable Adobe Audition as a SMPTE slave

1 Connect the SMPTE or MIDI output of the master device to the MIDI in socket of the PC.
2 Ensure that the frame rate of the master device matches the frame rate used by the Adobe Audition session. Right click over the Display Time window to see frame options.
3 Enable the PC as SMPTE Slave by choosing SMPTE Slave Enable from the Options menu in the multitrack view or by pressing F7 on the keyboard.
4 Set the master device running.
5 Adobe Audition will play back automatically from 0:00:00:00 or will wait for a valid offset before playback. Set playback offset in Advanced Session Properties.

MIDI commands are echoed in the bottom left border in the status window.

SMPTE offset

It is very unusual for both the session and the movie to start at 00:00:00:00 exactly. More likely is that the movie soundtrack needs to wait for titles or headers. At the video playback device note the SMPTE time at the point just before the soundtrack should begin. The enter that value in the SMPTE offset value in Advanced Session Properties. (Ctl+P) Adobe Audition will delay playback until the offset value is received.

Use SMPTE settings in Settings>Device Properties when troubleshooting sync problems between master and slave devices. The two most useful values in this dialog are Stopping Time and Slack time. If synching the PC with an older machine the Slack Time value allows for drift in the SMPTE code before Adobe Audition makes a guess and repositions the playback cursor to where it thinks it should be. Stopping Time allows Adobe Audition to keep going for a short period of time in case of dropouts or some other failure when reading time code.

Tip

Accidentally choosing a frame rate of 29.97FPS (SMPTE Drop Frame) causes SMPTE to drop three frames each minute. This will cause errors in playback *no matter* how lag or slack times are set. This setting caused me much frustration until I figured out what I was doing wrong and swapped to a standard 25FPS.

MIDI triggering

Any MIDI controller device (keyboard, guitar, drums, etc.) can be used to control features and functions including controlling playback, recording, effects, etc.

1   Ensure that the default MIDI In (recording) device shown in Options>Device Properties is the device that your MIDI equipment is connected to.
2   Choose Options>Keyboard Shortcuts from the menu bar and choose the type of controller you need (transport, effects, file, etc.) from the drop down box (Figure 6.1).
3   Use the mouse to click on any command name in the list and enter properties for the command in the right hand side of the dialog box.
4   Press any key on a MIDI keyboard connected to the soundcard to insert note and channel values for the shortcut assigned to the selected command.

Figure 6.1
Choose the type of controller you need from the drop down box

The MIDI note and channel appears in the MIDI trigger column alongside any enabled command. Each command may be enabled for Edit View, Multitrack View or both views by using the buttons just above the Shortcut column in this dialog.

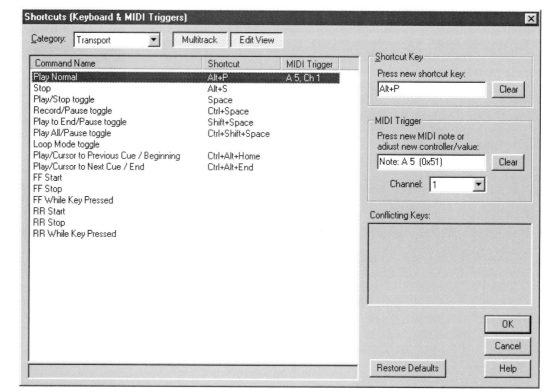

If the MIDI triggering appears not to work it may be that these options are incorrect. Finally the MIDI triggering needs to be enabled in either Edit View or Multitrack View for Adobe Audition to accept commands from the MIDI device. MIDI reception can be confirmed by looking at the lower left corner of the Adobe Audition status bar. A MIDI Triggering message can be seen followed by real time MIDI information whenever a key is pressed. If no real time information can be seen then Adobe Audition is not receiving information from the external device or sound card. In this case the connections and settings must be checked.

Tip

MIDI triggering must be enabled for each command in turn as there are different properties for each item.

Using the PC as a SMPTE slave to external device

Maximise the potential of all your legacy sequencing and recording equipment by enabling Adobe Audition as a 'slave' to an external sequencer (could even be another computer) In this scenario the PC is used simply as a remote MTR (Multitrack Tape Recorder) slaved via SMPTE over MTC to an external sequencer. When used this way Adobe Audition can concentrate on what it does best (be a great audio recorder) while leaving the boring MIDI sequencing stuff to another machine.

1 Switch to Multitrack View.
2 Connect MIDI out of the SMPTE master device to the MIDI in of the PC.
3 Set Adobe Audition to function as SMPTE slave by choosing Options>SMPTE Slave Enable from the menu bar. The words 'Opened MIDI Input Sync/Trigger' will appear in the lower right hand corner of the Adobe Audition window.
4 Send SMPTE code to Adobe Audition via MIDI.
5 Adobe Audition will start and chase the SMPTE code.

With Adobe Audition working as SMPTE or MIDI slave it's easy to program MIDI using the external equipment while recording high quality audio using the PC. The technique is a little old school but many people suspect MIDI timing on the PC isn't as rock solid as it should be and simply prefer the dedicated clock of external MIDI devices. Add to this the benefits of not tying system resources up with additional software, increased stability, the advanced MIDI functions of certain older 8bit software etc. etc.

To use the PC as the SMPTE master simply turn the connections on their head and connect the MIDI output of the PC to the MIDI input of the SMPTE Slave Device.

Remixing legacy recordings from tape

Utilising SMPTE sync can help solve a recently recurring problem, e.g: You have an old eight track multitrack recorder and some valuable recordings which you'd like to clean up and remix in the digital domain. The problem is that while it is possible to simply make four stereo passes into Adobe Audition, all four will be out of sync because varying motor speed and tape stretch mean that each pass will drift out of time. The solution is to lose one of the eight tracks, perhaps a backing vocal or percussion part that can easily be replaced. Using an external SMPTE generator stripe the newly created free track with SMPTE along the length of the tape. Enable

SMPTE slave and connect the MIDI out of the external sync box to MIDI in of the PC. The SMPTE code will have to be translated by the sync box into SMPTE or MTC over MIDI. With the SMPTE timing locked to the tape Adobe Audition will follow the timing drift accurately and the transfer can be achieved.

Creating markers for video 'spot effects'

Creating spot effects or synchronising speech to film requires the insertion of cues either as the video is playing or when playback has stopped (press F8 to manually insert a cue at any time). Use the Zoom to Selection button on the transport bar to close right in on any section of playback. Pressing the Fast Forward or Rewind button on the transport bar enables 'scrubbing' over any small section. Choose SMPTE (24fps) by right clicking over the display time window and enable snapping to Cues only (Edit>Snapping). Waveblocks can then be aligned with sample accuracy to any point in the video.

Remote control devices

If you own a Mackie, Tascam US224/ US428 or Event Ezbus USB control board, you may control a selection of Adobe Audition functions using the controls on the remote board rather than the computer keyboard. This is enables controlling of volume, pan and other values within the software through 'real' physical hardware faders and other control surfaces. Controlling the software in this way removes the necessity for the home musician to use the QWERTY keyboard and mouse to control the software. Guitar players are often bothered by the noise created through EMI (Electro Magnetic Interference) produced by computer monitors. Placing the controls away from the computer means less noise and also more room for guitars and amps etc. Options for configuring the external control device are found in the Ext Controller tab under Device Properties from the Options menu on the toolbar.

Red Rover

The Red Rover is a USB remote control device developed and produced by Syntrillium. Although an option to configure the Red Rover exists within Adobe Audition, it is not known whether these devices are still available.

Edit View

Multitrack View enables multiple waveforms to be laid end to end and tied together to create arrangements. Effects and other changes are non-destructive in the multitrack view. That is the changes are saved in the .ses file not the individual waveforms. Waveforms can also be recorded and played in the Edit View (F12). In this view only one waveform can be played back at a time even though many waveforms can be open in many Edit view workspaces in a session. The ability to make highly accurate, high quality changes to the waveform itself is the function of the Edit view. Adobe Audition is able to load waveform files saved by every PC Audio application.

Figure 7.1
A stereo waveform loaded in the Edit View.

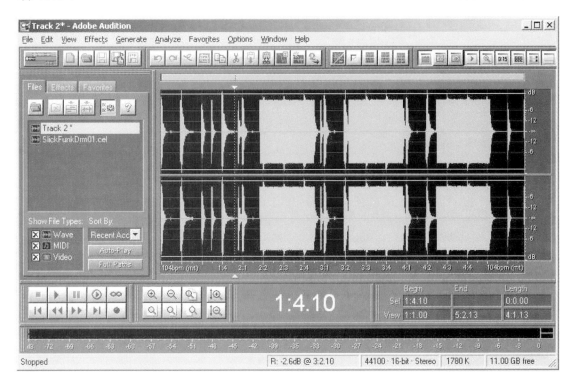

Navigating the Edit View

Transport and zoom controls

Controls for moving forwards, backwards, playing a waveform etc. are called the Transport controls and are placed on the Transport Bar below the waveform display. The transport bar has familiar buttons and functions enabling it to be easily understood;

- Stop
- Play
- Pause
- Play to end
- Play looped
- Go to beginning
- Rewind
- Fast-forward
- Go to end
- Record

The transport controls are situated in the lower left-hand corner of the main view. The controls are mainly intuitive with one or two exceptions,

Figure 7.2
The transport controls

Go to End

Causes the program to continue playing after it has reached the extreme right hand edge of the screen. If play alone is used playback will stop when the playback cursor reaches the edge of the screen.

Play Looped

Loops either the visible area of the waveform, or the selected area of the waveform until the stop button is pressed.

There are eight zoom buttons situated to the right of the Transport buttons. These are:

Zoom out	Zoom out fractionally
Zoom In	Zoom in fractionally
Zoom Full	Zooms all the way out to show the entire session or waveform within the window
Zoom to selection	Expand the current selection to fill the entire window. If no selection is made zooms in on the position of the playback cursor
Zoom to left of selection	Sets playback cursor to extreme left of selection. If entire waveform is not in view moves view to extreme left
Zoom to right of selection	Sets playback cursor to extreme right of selection. If entire waveform is not in view moves view to extreme right
Zoom in vertically	Enlarges the waveform display vertically
Zoom out vertically	Shrinks the waveform display vertically

Info

It's easy to overlook the very useful shuttle function. As the sample is playing in waveform view, Left click either the fast-forward, or fast rewind button to shuttle over the waveform. Right click to select shuttle speed.

Progressively clicking on the Zoom To Selection button zooms right in on the waveform until individual samples appear as lines between small squares. Right click on any square to see the sample value for easy editing, or the squares may be dragged around the waveform for precise editing.

Playback cursor

The playback cursor is always over the point within the waveform at which the sample currently being reproduced is stored. In other words it displays where along the waveform the playback is coming from. The playback cursor will move along the waveform when the fast forward or rewind buttons are pressed or it can simply be dragged along the waveform by the yellow handle at top and bottom. Playback always starts from the location of the playback cursor. To make the cursor jump from any point right back to the beginning of the waveform, simply press the Esc key on the keyboard.

Time window

Shows elapsed time at the current location of the playback cursor. Time is displayed in a number of different ways including Compact Disc format (75fps), SMPTE, and samples. The default setting is minute, second and decimal fractions of a second. Toggle between display formats by double clicking on the time ruler. Right click the time ruler to display additional options. Any time display format may be used at any time in either waveform or multitrack view. For instance if working in bars and beats you find that the resolution is not fine enough for editing in Edit View you may simply switch to Decimal until you wish to return to working in Bars and Beats.

Display Time Format

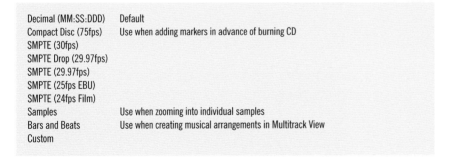

Custom time display format is set using Options>Settings in the General tab.

Time display fields

Display beginning, end, or length information for the entire waveform or a selected view. Left or right click inside the Time Display Field to manually adjust the values in these fields.

> **Tip**
>
> Press and hold the Alt key while using the up, down, left and right keyboard arrows to zoom vertically and horizontally.

Figure 7.3
The default setting of the Time window is minute, second and decimal fractions of a second.

Ruler bar

The time ruler is a simple ruler calibrated depending on the format chosen for the Time Display Window. Left click and drag along the ruler to move along the wave-form in either Multitrack or Edit view. Alternatively right click over the ruler or double left click on the ruler to toggle through the time format options.

Figure 7.4
The time ruler.

Level meters

The Level meters indicate amplitude received by Adobe Audition from the sound-card. Right click over the level meter to choose range and Peak Options. Input level above 0dB causes the clip indicators to illuminate. Adjust the level coming into your sound card from your external sound source until the level meter no longer meets the extreme right hand side of the window (0dB). Double click the red 'clip indicators' to clear. Right click over the level meters for options related to this feature. Default settings are 120dB range with dynamic peaks. Many users prefer a 60dB or 45dB range. If the level meters appear to be set wrongly or are clipping too early right click over the meter and toggle Adjust For DC setting.

Figure 7.5
The Level meters.

> **Tip**
>
> Remember that it is not possible to control how much level Adobe Audition receives from the sound card from within the program. Use the volume properties box or the utilities that come with your sound card in conjunction with your external sound source to ensure that the clip indicators do not illuminate.

Status bar

The status bar shows easy to understand information relating to file size file time, free space etc. Various options may be chosen from the right click menu. The most useful option – Data under cursor - is not enabled by default. Data under cursor shows information for the sample immediately under the mouse cursor, not the playback cursor. Right click over the status bar for options.

Figure 7.6
The status bar.

> **Tip**
>
> Press the ESC on the keyboard to place the playback cursor at the beginning of the waveform in Edit View.

Vertical zoom

The vertical zoom ruler is situated at the extreme right hand side of the waveform. By default the vertical zoom ruler indicates values in decibels. Right clicking over the vertical zoom ruler produces a menu from which other values may be chosen. The view as frequency option (Hz) is only enabled in the spectral view. Press Alt+ up arrow or Alt + down arrow to vertically zoom in or out of the waveform.

Figure 7.7
The vertical zoom ruler.

Navigating the toolbars and menu bars above the waveform display in Edit View

Switch view button

In Edit View switch to Multitrack View or in Multitrack View switch to Edit View. The keyboard F12 duplicates this action.

Display range bar

Adobe Audition can display all or just part of a waveform. The range bar shrinks or expands until it fills the entire length of the bar. When the entire bar is green the entire length of the waveform is visible.

To explore this feature, click on the Zoom Out Full Both Axis button in the transport bar. The display range bar is now solid green from left to right across the entire length of the bar. Now click the Zoom to Selection button once. The display range bar shrinks to show green only across about a third of the length of the bar. This indicates that the current view is only about a third of the total waveform. The display range bar has a couple of interesting attributes; left clicking and dragging on the centre of the green bar enables smooth scrolling over the entire waveform. Left click and drag the right and left leading edges of the display range bar to quickly zoom in or out of the waveform. Right click the display range bar to view options. A pale section of the display range bar indicates that a range is selected. The display range bar is also a floating window and can be moved and docked elsewhere if you prefer.

Figure 7.8
The Display range bar shrinks or expands until it fills the entire length of the bar

Menus and toolbars

Toolbars are groups of buttons reproducing each of the functions available from the menu bar. Right click over any button to reveal the toolbars menu.

Tip

If you find Toolbars are taking up too much room, right click over any toolbar button and choose the '1Row Limit' option.

File operations

File open

The standard Windows dialog allows any audio file to be previewed before loading into the waveform view. File information is shown in the right hand table of this dialog. If no information is available the program will attempt to guess the sample rate and frequency. Valid waveforms without header data (such as files saved on a Mac and burnt to CD) can be opened successfully using the default 'Intel' option when interpreting raw data.

1 Start Adobe Audition, and open one of these system sounds (File, Open).

2 Press the spacebar or the 'Play' button.

3   The level meters follow the amplitude of the waveform under the playback cursor.

Auto playing (auditioning) sounds from the File Open dialog

It's easy to hear audio files without having to open and close each one. Make sure the option for 'Autoplay' is checked within the File Open dialog box and simply click on any file to hear it. The default device for this is the same device used in the Edit view.

The waveform is shown as a green shape on a black background. Press play on the transport bar or press the keyboard space bar to start playback. During playback the yellow playback cursor moves along the waveform until it reaches the end. Click inside the waveform at any point to change the place that the playback cursor will start playing from. Click the extreme upper (left) or lower (right) limits of the waveform to hear just one channel of a stereo waveform. The cursor changes into a small L or small R to indicate that just one side of the stereo waveform is being selected. Click the centre line to return to normal view. Underneath the waveform is the time ruler calibrated in hours, minutes, and seconds. To the right of the waveform display is the Amplitude ruler. The amplitude of the waveform can be measured in Samples, Decibels, Percentage or Normalised Values. Decibel is the default. To change the scale of this ruler right click inside the Amplitude ruler and select from the drop-down menu. The green line at the centre of the waveform display indicates no value, or the quietest part of waveform. Above and below this line the waveform will playback louder until eventually the sound is clipped where the waveform meets the boundary line (0dB)

> ### Tip
>
> If no sound appears on playback check the device options in Options>Device Properties. Use the device properties dialog to choose which sound card or sound card output is used by default for playback. If necessary, change the device order until your preference appears as the default device in the Wave Out tab. Change the device order by pressing the 'change' button within the dialog box.

Selecting and editing the new waveform

The waveform is simply a graphical representation of the sounds digitised by the sound card then stored as numbers inside the computer. Viewed from left to right the largest parts of the waveform indicate high amplitude or values (loud sounds). Values exceeding 0dB will appear above or below the blue line at the upper and lower reaches of the waveform display. Data appearing here will be 'clipped' causing the clip indicators to illuminate. The waveform may be viewed at almost any resolution from the entire waveform to just one sample. Use the 'Zoom In To Selection' button to zoom right in on the waveform. It's possible to zoom right in until the wave appears as a single line segmented with squares. The portion of the line between two squares is a single sample. If you chose to record at 44100 kHz there will be over 44,000 of these segments for every second of music. Zoom To Selection can be very useful, especially for removing pops and clicks.

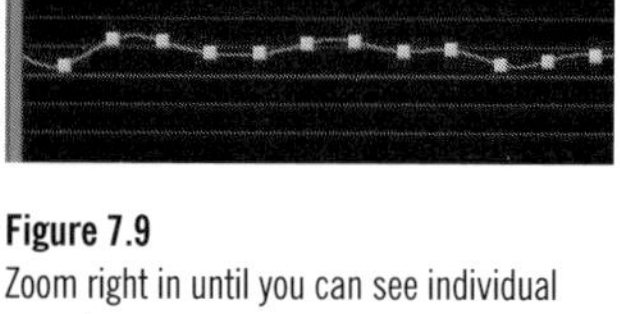

> ### Tip
>
> Adobe Audition is the best option for your default waveform player as it is able to open, load and edit files from almost every PC audio application including Cakewalk, Cubase VST, N-Tracks, etc.

> ### Tip
>
> Playback will stop when the cursor reaches the end of the current view (the extreme right hand of the window). Use the Play To End button instead of the Play button to continue playback past the end of the current view.

Figure 7.9
Zoom right in until you can see individual samples.

Clipped portions of a waveform are reproduced as noise. Unlike a tape recording that can sound 'hot' if the recording is made at a high level, digital clipping doesn't yet have any commercial value and should be avoided. Look carefully at the input levels of your soundcard and make adjustments until the incoming signal always sits comfortably below the red line.

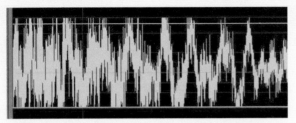

Figure 7.10
This waveform has been overamplified. The clipped areas of the wave above the boundary lines will sound as distortion.

Selecting a range

Click and drag over any part of the waveform to select. If the Zoom to Selection button is now pushed the view will expand to show that area of the waveform only. Effects are applied only to the visible area of the waveform. Playback will start at the playback cursor and stop at the end of the selected range unless the Play to End button is pushed. The selected area may now be repeated (looped) indefinitely by using the loop button on the transport bar.

Shrink or grow the left side of the selected area using the keyboard shortcuts.

L	Right side grow
K	Right side shrink
H	Left side grow
J	Left side shrink

Be careful, as pressing the delete key will immediately delete the selected area.

The yellow range handles at top and bottom of the Edit View may also be dragged to shrink or grow the selected area.

Working with a selected area

The selected area of a waveform can be saved, cut, copied and pasted, etc. just like any other data. Click the 'Zoom To Selection' button on the transport bar to expand the selected area to fill the waveform view. You can now work on this area only. Caution. By default effects, etc. are applied only to the visible area of the waveform. In other words if only the first third of a waveform is visible in the waveform view and an effect or any other process is applied to the waveform only the area of the waveform visible in the waveform view will be processed. This is important for instance if a vocal mixdown wave has been loaded and needs to be processed. It's possible to forget that only a portion of the waveform is visible and so any effects would be applied only to the first third of the vocal mixdown. Use the green 'range

To enable effects over the entire waveform, even if only a selection is visible choose 'Entire Wave' from the Default Selection Options in the Settings dialog.

If the Extend Selection option is chosen in Options>Settings> General the selection may simply be extended by right-click and dragging the cursor over the waveform. If this method is chosen the pop-up menu may be revealed by pressing the Cntrl key while right-clicking.

bar' above the waveform to determine whether the entire wave is visible before creating a beautiful vocal sound that will only be heard for the first minute of the song! Effects are applied to just the selected area even if the option for Entire Wave is chosen in Default Selection Range in the Properties dialog (F4) This is because that option only applies during editing of complete waveforms, not a selection.

Save selection
To save only the selected area of the loaded wave as a new file choose File>Save Selection. Press Ctrl and T (Trim) to discard the unselected areas of the waveform. The selected area can also be reloaded as a brand new waveform (Edit, Copy To New).

Copying and pasting data
Adobe Audition offers five clipboards for copying data between waveforms. Press Ctrl + 1 to Ctrl + 5 to select each clipboard (the current clipboard is shown in the status bar) or Ctrl + 6 to choose the Windows clipboard. Data is kept in the clipboard until the program is closed. Data is copied to a clipboard using File>Copy or File>Cut from the menu bar. Copying data leaves the selected area intact. Cutting data removes the selected area from the waveform. If no area is selected, only the currently shown area of the wave (visible in the view) is copied. Choose Edit>Select Entire Wave (or press Ctl+A) to copy the entire waveform to the clipboard. Remember to recall the correct clipboard before pasting.

Paste (Ctl + V)
Inserts the contents of the clipboard at the current position of the playback cursor.

Paste to New (Ctl + Shift + N)
Loads the contents of the clipboard into the Edit View as a new file.

Mix Paste (Ctl + Shift + V)
Pastes the currently selected clipboard at the playback cursor over any existing data. The clipboard data is merged with the existing data according to selections made in the mix paste dialog. The volume slider values are shown as percentages so 100 will paste the new data over the existing data at the same level as the original. Choosing 'Loop Paste' repeats the contents of the clipboard as many times as you wish. Contents may be pasted from the last used clipboard (close dialog and press Ctrl + 1 through 5 to select another clipboard), the Windows clipboard or from a file.

Insert	Inserts clipboard data at playback cursor
Overlap	Mixes contents of clipboard with existing data at levels set with slider
Replace	Replaces samples to length of contents of clipboard
Modulate	Waveform inherits amplitude of contents of clipboard
Crossfade	Fades the clipboard data in and out to the value specified here

Open Append
Choosing File>Open Append causes the program to insert another file at the very end of the currently open file. Mix Paste (Ctl + Shift + V) duplicates this function and offers options such as amplitude, insert, overlap, etc. for the pasted data.

Saving waveform files

Waveforms may be saved in any of 18 file formats suitable for nearly every computing platform. The most common of these and the default is Windows PCM. A file in this format is saved as pure un-compressed data. Additional non-audio information such as time and date etc. may also be saved along with the audio data. In the Edit view choose View>Info to view and edit this information. Each file format has advanced options relative to that format available through the 'Advanced' button in the Save File dialog. Other useful file formats include the Apple AIFF format, the Sound Blaster .VOC format and Real Audio .RA format. Save your files as Windows PCM 32 Bit float (Type 1) for the highest quality with the least problems within the PC environment. Use F1 to see detailed descriptions of each save format.

File>Save and File>Save As

These two menu items function exactly as in any other program running in the Windows environment. However some useful features are accessed in this direction.

Options

Within the save dialog is a drop down menu list containing file filters (*.flt) and an Options button. If your waveform is intended to remain stored in your system or may need further editing, choose the default option; Windows PCM (*.wav) as this option ensures that the waveform is stored in the most compatible format for Adobe Audition and other programs. Most formats have additional options found under the options button in the Save As dialog. Adobe Audition offers the ability to save in more file formats than any other PC Audio Editing suite.

Audio formats supported by Adobe Audition

64 Bit Doubles	*.dbl	8 Byte doubles in Binary Form
8-Bit Signed	*.sam	MOD compatible format (22050Hz)
Amu-Law Wave	*.wav	Telephony only (CCITT standard G.711)
ACM Waveform	*.wav	Microsoft Audio Compression Manager
Amiga IFF-8SVX	*.iff *.svx	Commodore Amiga 8 Bit Mono
Apple AIFF	*.aif *.snd	Macintosh compatible
ASCII Text Data	*.txt	Standard Text Format
Audition Loop	*.cel	Loop file in enhanced MP3 format
Creative Sound Blaster	*.voc	Creative Labs Sound Blaster software
Dialogic ADPCM	*.vox	Telephony only (no header)
Diamondware Digitized	*.dwd	Game sound designers format
DVI/IMA ADPCM	*.wav	International Multimedia Association alternative to Microsoft ADPCM
Microsoft ADPCM	*.wav	Microsoft compressed audio
MPEG 3 (FhG)	*.mp3	Popular distribution form
Next/Sun	*.au *.snd	NeXT/Sun format used in Java apps
SampleVision	*.smp	Turtle Beach Samplevison
Windows PCM	*.wav	Default
PCM Raw Data	*.pcm *.raw	Raw data (unknown format)

The help file contains detailed scientific information about these formats and the ways in which Adobe Audition interacts with other software through them.

> ### Tip
>
> A loaded waveform is automatically converted into an internal format. On saving the waveform is converted back to one of the standard formats. Windows PCM is the default for PC recording.
>
> Some users report that data compression and file management tools have peculiar effects on audio data. Although the jury is still out about the true effects of compression on your audio it's still too much of a risk to take with your precious audio files in my opinion. If you can afford to, keep your WAVs as they were recorded even if it does mean using a little hard disk space or some blank CD Roms.

Save as
Returns to the folder from where the waveform was originally loaded.

Save copy as
Remembers the last place that you saved a waveform to. Intended for use when saving a copy of the file to an alternative location instead of the location the file was loaded from.

> ### Back up!
>
> The time spent creating waveforms and sessions, the endless tweaking, collecting samples, loops and beats can't be reclaimed in the event of a disaster unless you have a good backup of your hard disk. Copy your data across to tape or CD-R after every session.

Partitioning the waveform using cues

Cues may be inserted at any point along the waveform or in a multitrack session. Once in place the markers have a wide variety of uses such as to identify different sections of the waveform, to mark pops and clicks, to automatically display and select ranges or to indicate where tracks are to start when converting to CD format. Every cue is automatically added to a Cue List where properties may be edited and given a meaningful label such as 'bad click'. Cues can be deleted, merged or even used to create new waveforms. Two or more cues may be merged together to form a Cue Range.

Creating a new cue
Press F8 at any time during playing or recording to enter a brand new cue. Single cues are indicated as small yellow arrows at the top of the waveform on the cue bar along with the default cue name. A cue range is created if F8 is pressed while an area of the waveform is selected. The Cue Range contains the selected area and is identified by two smaller half arrows; yellow indicating the start of the range, blue marking the end of the range. Use as many cues, markers and cue ranges as you need to in the waveform up to a maximum of 96 per wave.

> ### Tip
>
> se Edit>Snap to Cues to make working within the large waveform very easy. Placing cues at key points means the playback cursor will jump to the next cue when the Zoom Left or Zoom Right button is pushed.

Figure 7.11
Three cue types have been created in this waveform.

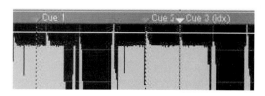

Cue lists

Each cue and cue range is added to a Cue List. Cue Lists are saved with the wave-form and each waveform has it's own Cue List. To see the Cue List select View, Cue List from the menu bar or press Alt + 8 on the keyboard (Figure 7.12). Each cue is shown in the list, identified by a label and a beginning time. Clicking each field in the dialog box is a simple way to edit label and time values. Use the mouse to click the button 'Edit Cue Info' to reveal the editable fields. The Autoplay button will cause Adobe Audition to start playback from the begin time of each highlighted cue.

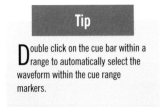

Tip

Double click on the cue bar within a range to automatically select the waveform within the cue range markers.

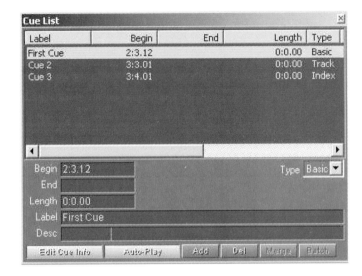

Figure 7.12
The Cue List showing cues within the loaded waveform.

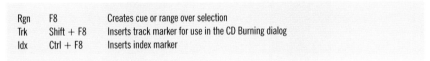

Rgn	F8	Creates cue or range over selection
Trk	Shift + F8	Inserts track marker for use in the CD Burning dialog
Idx	Ctrl + F8	Inserts index marker

Each cue and range is named automatically, however meaningful descriptions such as a song title can be attached if text is entered in the label and description boxes in the Cue List dialog.

Cue ranges

Selecting a section of the wave, then pressing Add while the Cue List is open also creates a new range in the Cue List. Double clicking a Cue Range takes you to and highlights that selection in the waveform. Left click and drag over one or more entries in the Cue List to merge those entries together. Please note, this dialog box has no undo feature. Save your work regularly!

Batch processing in the Cue List

It's very simple to split a large waveform into sections or separate files. From the Cue List click and drag, control-click or shift-click to select one or more Cue ranges, then press the 'Batch' button to bring up the batch process dialog box (Figue 7.13).

Figure 7.13
The batch editing dialog. Remember batch editing of cues can only be performed on Cue Ranges.

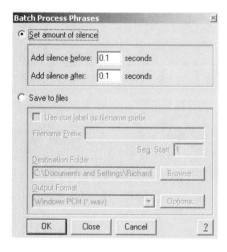

Splitting the waveform by inserting silence

This technique creates easily identifiable sections within the large waveform. Use small values (0.5 seconds or less) to ensure that the waveform does not grow considerably in length.

Tip

Create small 0.5 sec spaces between each range before batch saving to ensure no information is missed from the beginning or end of the new file

Batch saving of cues to files

This important time-saving technique saves each section or song as a separate file.

1 Merge individual cues to create cue ranges.
2 With cue ranges set press batch button in Cue List.
3 Choose Save To Files.
4 Set filename prefix to any meaningful name, e.g Loop.
5 Use the '?' placeholder to mark the point in the file name where you would like a number to be saved in the filename, e.g; loop?
6 Set destination folder and format options.
7 Press OK to save each cue range as a new waveform file.

Play List

With a meaningful list of cues complete with names and descriptions in the Cue List, a Play List can be created to play each cue, either in order or out of order. Additionally each instance can be repeated. It's possible to make short musical pieces in this way. Both the Cue List and the Play List are floating windows so they may be open at the same time and left open while the waveform is edited.

1 Use View>Show Play List to see the Play List window (Figure 7.14).
2 Arrange the desktop so that the Waveform, the Cue List and the Play List are all visible. The Cue List has a list of cues.
3 Click on any cue in the Cue List and click 'Insert Cue' in the Play List window.

4 A new entry is created in the Play List window with the title of the Cue. The end of the Play List is now highlighted.

5 Choose another cue from the Cue List and click to select.

6 Press 'Add Before' in the Play List to create another entry in the Play List containing the next cue. Do this as many times as necessary.

Cues can be repeated and looped and multiple instances of the same cue can be added to the list. Finally click the first entry in the Play List and press Play. Each cue will be played in the order of the Play List. The Auto-cue feature will play the highlighted cue in the list only. The Play List is saved along with the waveform in Microsoft PCM format but not if the waveform is saved in any of the 'lossy' formats (MP3 etc.) Although the Play List can be used to play sections of the wave in the wrong order it is completely 'non-destructive' meaning that no matter what order you create in the Play List, the waveform itself will remain intact.

Auto-cue

Making cue-lists for long passages of speech can easily be achieved with the Auto-cue feature. This automates the procedure of creating Cue Lists by scanning selected ranges of the waveform looking for areas where the amplitude dips below a pre-set threshold for more than a hundred milliseconds.

To use auto-cue to create a cue range from a phrase in the waveform
Drag Select over an area of the waveform that contains the phrase and choose from the following menu items.

Adjust Selection To Phrase
If a range has been selected over an area of speech, this option will adjust the boundaries of the highlighted area inwards after and before digital silence

Find Phrases and Mark

Adobe Audition will look for the points of lowest amplitude within the selected area and create a cue range from this. Although the menu item is called 'Find Phrases And Mark' this feature will only create one cue range even if two or three distinct phrases are within the selected area.

Find Beats and Mark

To detect each phrase automatically choose 'Find Beats and Mark' This feature causes the program to scan the waveform and place a cue marker at the front of each phrase. However, it doesn't join the markers to create ranges. To do this, open the Cue Window and shift-click or ctrl-click two or more items in the Cue List. With more than one cue highlighted the 'Merge' button will become available. Press the merge button to create a range from two cues. Add Labels and Descriptions to the cue range as usual.

Auto-cue settings

Define silence and audio in this dialog so Auto-cue can make decisions regarding which areas in the waveform are speech or not. If the waveform is well recorded the definition of silence can be set very low to around −80dB. However if the waveform contains background noise the threshold must be raised to around −34dB or so depending on the amplitude and frequency the background noise. If words and phrases are skipped or removed raise or lower these values accordingly. Use the Find Levels function to scan the waveform and estimate thresholds automatically

Trim Digital Silence

When the lower threshold has been calculated correctly this function will remove any areas below the lower threshold and defined as digital silence.

Using cues to create loops in the Edit View

Contemporary and Top 40 music is very often based wholly on repeated sections of a drum or bass pattern called loops. The loop is simply a short section of another record or sometimes a specially recorded piece of music, cycling round indefinitely. Creating a waveform with seamless beginning and ends is called looping. The short waveform itself is the loop. Cues and ranges are used to mark start and end points when creating loops or samples from within a larger waveform. In order to used looped drum patterns or phrases within the Multitrack View it is necessary to create the looped section in the Edit View first. Loops may be individually saved to new files or encoded in MP3 or other formats for use in other audio programs such as Fruity Loops etc. CD ROM disks can also be created that will play back in your sampler just like pre-recorded disks.

It's easy to playback any section of a wave as a loop in the Edit View. Use the mouse to press the loop (infinity ∞) button on the transport bar. The selected area of the wave will now playback as a loop. Pressing the spacebar now stops or starts playback in loop mode, to turn off the loop you must use the mouse to press the play button on the transport bar.

Making a simple repeated playback loop from an area of a larger waveform

1   Load or record a waveform containing a drum pattern.
2   Click and drag over the waveform to select an area just a little bigger than necessary (Figure 7.15). (Press ESC if you need to deselect and return to the beginning of the waveform).

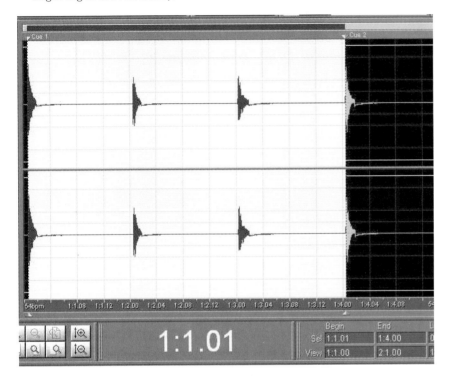

Figure 7.15
Select an area just a little bigger than necessary

3   Use the 'Zoom To Selection' tool to expand that area to fill the screen.
4   Play the wave again.
5   Look at the waveform, you should be able to see the beginning of the downbeat, it's usually a loud sound.
6   Play the wave again until you can identify it.
7   Click inside the waveform at the point where the down beat just starts.
8   Play the waveform again to make sure the yellow marker is in exactly the right place.
9   On the menu bar find Edit> Find Beats>Find Next Beat Right. The selected range will expand to include the next beat detected in the waveform.
10 Loop the selected area by pressing the loop button on the transport bar.
11 As the loop is playing use Edit>Find Beats to extend the range until your loop sounds OK

Tip

Finding beats accurately is much easier if snapping is disabled by removing all the tick marks in Edit>Snapping. CEL files contain markers for each event within the cel.

Creating a loop using cues

Find next beat is great if you have a cool clear drum pattern but to work it needs each beat to be well defined. A noisy guitar riff, or vinyl drum break needs a little more work. Use markers to find the approximate beginning and end of the loop before defining the exact selected area precisely using the cursor keys.

1 Select the area of the recording that contains the loop you want to snatch.
2 Play the waveform, and press F8 on the downbeat at the beginning and end of the loop. Don't worry if the cues aren't exactly on the downbeat but try and make the first cue 'early' and the last cue 'late' to create more room for editing in the next step.
3 Open the Cue List (View>Cue List or press Alt +8).
4 Merge the two cues to form a range.
5 Double-click this range to highlight it.
6 Press the loop button on the transport bar to loop the highlighted area.
7 While the loop plays use the H,J,K and L keys on the keyboard to adjust the size of the selected range.
8 Adjust the size of the range until the loop is exactly is you want it.

Saving the looped section

The highlighted range may now be saved as a brand new file by choosing File>Save Selection from the menu bar.

Using external devices to aid loop creation

External MIDI devices can be used to trigger playback. This can be useful when creating loops to fit alongside existing loops. For instance older samplers can be difficult to use when truncating samples. It is much easier to create a loop of exactly the right length before sampling into the external device.

1 Use Adobe Audition to find the start of the loop or phrase for sampling into the external device.
2 Use F6 to enable MIDI triggering and set MIDI trigger using Options>Keyboard Shortcuts.
3 In Keyboard Shortcuts find the Play/Stop Toggle command and enable the MIDI trigger for that command. Choose appropriate MIDI channel and note for your system.
4 Set your external MIDI sequencer or software to trigger both the external sampler and Adobe Audition simultaneously.
5 With both devices firing simultaneously it's now simple to create a loop or one-shot sample of exactly the right length.

When the phrase or loop is ready simply route the output of the sound card to the input of the sampler.

Saving selections as a new file

Cues are often inserted at the beginning and the end of sections or songs within the waveform. These cues can then be used as markers for use when saving a selection of the waveform only.

1 Play the whole file from beginning to end and add cue markers (F8) to mark each section.
2 Set snap to cues (Edit>Snapping) and drag select between the first pair of markers.
3 With the selected area highlighted choose File>Save Selection from the menu bar and save the selected area with a new file name.

The selected area may now be deleted or you may move on within the file to the next set of cues. Whatever you do your first range is now securely saved to the hard disk. Two cues may be merged to form a Cue Range. Each range can be selected and saved as a new file. This procedure is very useful if a large waveform has been created containing many songs or sections which require saving individually. See the section on Cue Lists earlier in this chapter.

Edit > Copy to New

The selected area is loaded into a new file within the current session. In this case the file is not saved immediately but is loaded for further editing. Although the source waveform appears to disappear it is still in memory and may be retrieved at any time by choosing the file name from the Window menu. Files not saved yet are simply called Untitled followed by a number. The currently loaded file is indicated with an asterisk (*).

Edit > Trim

Removes any part of the waveform outside the currently selected range. May be used to trim the empty start and end section of a waveform.

Saving as Cel loop format (*.cel)

Cel files contain both audio data and markers to enable the loop to be imported seamlessly into future Adobe Audition multitrack sessions.

1   Place the cursor over the area of the waveform where you wish the phrase or loop to start.
2   Left click and drag over a section of the waveform.
3   Press the play button on the transport bar, or press the spacebar on the keyboard to hear only the selected area of the wave.
4   Use Edit > Find Next Beat or Edit > Zero Crossings to tune the length of the loop until it sounds right. Use the H,J,K and L keys on the keyboard while the loop is playing to adjust the edges of the selection.
5   When the loop is seamless right-click over the selection and choose 'Trim' from the menu to remove the unused part of the waveform.
6   Right click over the trimmed waveform and choose Wave Properties from the menu.
7   In the Loop Info tab edit the values in the fields to suit your loop.
8   Use File > Save Selection to save.
9   Choose to save as a *.cel file.
10 Press the options key to see advanced options. Choose the default 128kbps Stereo (Internet).

The loop is now saved in a format suitable for distribution and for transmission to other users of Adobe Audition who may simply import the *.cel file into a new or existing session. The .cel file contains the waveform looping and playback properties of the original recording.

Non audio information saved with file

In the Wave Properties dialog are a number of text fields for copyright and other information. Simple information such as Waveform title and Artist, etc. can be noted here as well as more complex information such as loop information for samplers etc. MP3 (ID3) Tags are also completed in this dialog.

Text Fields Tab (Standard RIFF)

Display Title	Key Words	Digitizer	Creation Date *
Original Artist	Digitization Source	Source Supplier	Comments
Name	Original Medium	Copyright	Subject
Genre	Engineers	Software Package *	

Text Fields Tab (Radio Industry)

Description	Intro Time (ms/begin)	Agency
Advertiser	Sec Tone (ms/end)	Account Executive
Outcue	Producer	Creation Date *
Start Date	Talent	Comments
End Date	Category	Copy

Text Fields Tab (MP3 ID3 Tag)

Song Title	Genre	Track Number
Artist	Year *	
Album Name	Comments	

Loop Info

Required by the Multitrack View for enabling the waveform to loop. The loop info must be calculated correctly and the waveform must be saved before advanced loop properties such as auto time stretching can be enabled in the multitrack view. See the section on enabling looping in the Multitrack View for details.

EBU Extensions

Data within this section may be used by hardware which conforms to the EBU (European Broadcast Union) standards.

Sampler

Sample information is saved in the header of the .WAV file.

- Target Manufacturer. This field is not editable. Contains data created by external sampler when writing .wav if available.
- Target product Code, This field is not editable. Contains data created by external sampler when writing .wav if available.
- Sample Period. The sample rate is shown in this field. This is editable if you wish the target sampler to reproduce data at a different rate.
- MIDI Unity Note is where data enabling the host device to map the sample to the correct key or MIDI note is stored. If the sample is a musical one the Note value should be set to the unity note of the waveform (Adobe Audition will analyse and detect this if necessary). Use the Fine Tune function to bring the note exactly into tune.
- The SMPTE offset section is where SMPTE information for that waveform is stored. Set the SMPTE format and offset values to suit your environment.

Sampler loops

Sampler Loops may be used by hardware samplers when loading the waveform. Sampler Loops appear in the Cue List but Cues and Cue ranges do not appear in the Sampler Loops list. Loops have differing attributes such as Infinite Looping, number of loops, direction, etc. To create a loop;

1   Close the Wave Properties box.
2   Create a range within the waveform to loop seamlessly.
3   Right click over the waveform and choose Wave Properties from the menu or choose View>Wave Properties from the menu bar.
4   In the Sampler tab use the 'New' button to add the loop to the list and set attributes accordingly.

Recording single waveforms in the Edit View

Recording a waveform within the Edit View is as easy as connecting a sound source to the input of a sound card and pressing the red 'record' button on the transport bar.

File>New

If the Edit View is empty Adobe Audition will present a prompt asking for the sample rate and bit depth for the new file (Figure 7.16). Choose depending on the source and the quality that you wish for the new recording.

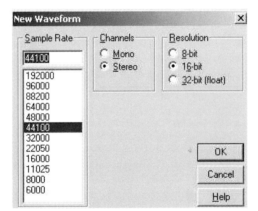

Figure 7.16
Adobe Audition asks for the sample rate and bit depth for the new file.

Table of commonly used formats

Sample Rate	Channels	Resolution	Result
192000	Stereo	32bit	For effects processing only
96000	Stereo	32bit	DVD quality with large file sizes. The 24/96 setting when used with a 24bit card
88200			
64000			
48000	Mono or stereo	32bit	Optimum middle ground trading off size against quality. Recommended for general waveform recording and editing.
44100	Mono or stereo	16bit	Many users default to this believing it to produce optimum (ie; CD quality) results. The capabilities of many soundcards well exceed this older standard. Pro engineers and audiophiles use this sample rate and bit depth only when producing audio for distribution. i.e; CD's and MP3's must be produced using data at this rate.
32000			
22050	Mono or stereo	16bit or lower	Low resolution (less detail) but useful for smaller file sizes
16000			
11025	Mono	16bit or 8bit	Real Audio, Telephony or data compression quality
8000	Mono	8bit	Smallest acceptable format for telephony only

If you want to take advantage of a brand new sound card with 24/96 capability you must record at 96kHZ using a bit depth of 32bits to capture all the information coming from the sound card. This format offers DVD quality audio at the expense of very large file sizes. Any format above 44.1/16bit must be downsampled eventually to meet the twenty-year-old CD standard. Commonly the slightly higher sample rate of 48kHZ is used at a bit depth of 32bits. This provides plenty of dynamic range without creating overlarge files difficult for the multitrack view to manipulate.

When to use 24/96?

If you imagine that the samples and sounds coming from most keyboards and tone modules have been sampled or downsampled to 44.1/16 there seems little point in trying to capture information that has already been lost. Likewise if you are ripping from a CD or taking samples from CD there's little point in recording at anything other than 44.1/16, which is the CD standard anyway. However if you are passing these sounds through another box such as a quality reverb you may want to enable 48/32 to capture the real time reverb tails generated by the outboard piece of equipment. To play devil's advocate, maybe the reverb is generating samples at 44.1/16 anyway in which case there's still little point! On the other hand if you have real musicians and good microphones recording at anything less than 24/96 seems criminal when the aim is to create a fantastic production. However, recording at this rate can cause problems when using the waveforms in Multitrack View as the extra large file sizes cause background mixing to slow right down. The middle ground of 48/32 captures everything coming from your professional sound card but doesn't make waveforms that are unwieldy. Of course as long as we are burning to CD the waveforms will have to be downsampled anyway but at least the effects and eq, etc, which have been applied will be the highest quality available. The bottom line is to choose your format according to your source.

After setting the options in the new file dialog Adobe Audition is almost ready to start recording. Before starting the new recording check the input levels are set correctly by pressing F10 on the keyboard and start your sound source. The level meter will show how much level is arriving at the input of the sound card. Optimum levels will peak at around –6dB. Levels meeting the right-hand side of the bar (0dB) will illuminate the Clip Level indicator to indicate that the level coming into the computer is too high and will cause the waveform to be clipped. To clear, click once in the Clip level indicator. Remember never to connect the input of your sound card to the speaker output of any amplifier; if you do this you'll destroy your sound card, and possibly your whole computer! Use line-out or headphone connections only.

Unlike a tape player it's not necessary to get as much level onto the hard disk as possible. As yet there's no such thing as warm 'hard disk compression'! If you overdrive the input of your sound card you'll hear a horrible noise called 'clipping'. Clipping is '..a phenomenon that occurs in digital audio when the amplitude value of a signal exceeds the maximum level that can be represented by the current bit resolution (i.e. 256 steps in 8-bit audio)'!. In other words the level going into a computer is too high. Although there is a repair effect for clipped audio, even a slightly clipped waveform is almost unusable. Turn the output of your sound source down or adjust settings in Windows mixer until the level meter goes no higher than –6dB. It's not possible within Adobe Audition to affect the amount of sound coming into the program. This may be done either with the Windows mixer or with the mixer application supplied with your sound card, depending on your model. If the input level is too high or too low use your Windows mixer to adjust the level until it is correct, this might mean adjusting the volume of the external sound source.

When you are ready to record press the red button on the transport bar or use the keyboard shortcut Ctrl + Spacebar to start the recording. Stop the recording by pressing the spacebar again. After a short while most people get used to simply using Ctrl –Spacebar instead of using the mouse. Adobe Audition will record for as long as the computer has storage space. This recorder isn't going to run out of tape! To see how much recording time is left right click on the status bar at the bottom right hand corner of the screen and choose 'Free Space (time)'. Available storage space is shown in minutes and seconds in the status bar. While recording it should be possible to clearly see the waveform being drawn on the screen. If not, (and if the level meters are moving indicating that something should be drawn on the screen) choose Options>Settings from the menu bar (or press F4). Within the settings dialog check 'Auto Update During Record' is selected. A flat green line and no indication on the level meters always means that data isn't arriving from the sound card.

Troubleshooting

Adobe Audition can't hear or play anything without a properly installed and configured sound card. Choose Options>Device Properties from the menu bar and ensure that your sound card appears within the Wave Out and Wave In tabs (Figure 7.17). Each sound card installed in the computer will appear in the drop down list. Visit Windows Control Panel>Settings>Multimedia if all sound card devices inside your computer do not appear in the Device Properties list and ensure that your card is installed correctly. If all sound cards are installed and listed correctly Adobe Audition will play back through the device selected for Edit View. Load any waveform into Edit View and start playback. Remember that 9/10 sound card problems can be resolved by removing all non-essential devices (modems, multi-head display adapters, etc) and most importantly *by double-checking that the connection to external amplification is actually plugged into the right socket!*

The order in which installed sound cards appear is not important in the Edit View as any card can be chosen as the Edit View device by selecting the required device in the list and enabling the option 'Use this device in Edit View' The device order is more important when working in multitrack view as Adobe Audition can use multiple devices in this view and so needs to be told which to use first. Multiple devices

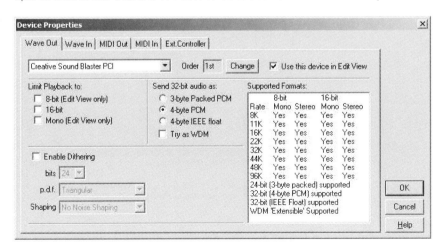

Figure 7.17
Ensure that your sound card appears within the Wave Out and Wave In tabs.

are not used in Edit View. Adobe Audition can only use one input or recording device in Edit View. The currently selected device is shown in the Wave In tab found within the Settings dialog box (F4). As with the playback device the Edit View device must be enabled b selecting the required device from the drop down list and enabling the 'Use this device in Edit View' option.

32bit float

Setting the new waveform to record at 32bit doesn't mean that your sound card is therefore recording at 32bits as well. The sound card is limited to the capabilities of the ADC (Analogue Digital Converters) on board the card. These may be sixteen, eighteen or even twenty-four bit. Adobe Audition merely receives the converted data from the sound card via the software driver. However, working in 32bits allows the program to create effects with twice as much depth as simply 16bits. It's good practise to convert every waveform you work on to 48/32 while editing. The resulting dynamic range will be greater, effects will sound finer and the overall quality of your waveform will be enhanced, even after downsampling in preparation for returning to CD quality. The important thing to remember is that the CD standard is 16bit recording at 44100 kHz. This means that a 32bit file must be downsampled and dithered to 16 bit before the CD can be burnt. Downsampling from 32 bits to 16 bits produces a much higher quality file than simply recording, editing and converting and burning all at 16 bit.

Level meters

Adobe Audition can only record data sent to it from a correctly installed sound card and verifying that the program is receiving this data is as simple as enabling the level meters. Press F10 to view level meters or choose View>Level Meters from the menu bar. Level meters always show playback in the Edit View. When playback is stopped pressing F10 will enable the Level Meters to show data received by the device chosen as the default device in the Device Properties>Wave In. If the level meters don't 'work' it always means that Adobe Audition isn't getting data from the sound card. If the default device for Edit View is correct Adobe Audition will always work properly – in fact it's the most reliable audio software available, that's why pro engineers and audio scientists all over the world rate it higher than any other.

- Check your connections
- Check the sound card is installed correctly (Windows System)
- Check the default device in Options>Settings

Connections to the computer

Connections can be confusing and aren't easy – particularly if you have one of those sound cards with all the connections round the back and under the desk! Most computer sound cards have 'mini' (3.5mm) stereo jacks for connections. Connecting leads must be placed in the correct socket or the computer won't function as expected. Creative Labs cards are almost standard now in most computers so I'm using their colour coding in this example.

- Connect a microphone only to the microphone input, normally coloured red.
- Line level instruments such as synths, etc. must be connected to the line input, normally coloured blue.
- Powered speakers are connected to the line output sockets, normally coloured green.
- Headphones are connected to the headphones output, normally coloured black.

Tip

One-minute of stereo waveform 16 bit data recorded at 44100 will take 10 megabytes of hard disk space. One-minute of stereo waveform 32 bit data recorded at 44100 KhZ takes 20 megabytes of hard disk space.

Playback will stop as soon as the playback cursor reaches the right hand edge of the current view. Press the play to end button to enable the playback cursor to travel past the right hand edge of the view. Don't blame the software!

Some cards have a front panel featuring 'traditional' 1/4 inch guitar phone jacks for use with line level equipment and microphones, etc. Check your documentation for instructions on how to utilise these features.

Info

Note: Record decks without an internal pre-amplifier must be connected to an additional pre-amp or amp with line out (tape record) connections. Without a pre-amp the signal from the record deck will not sound as expected within the computer. Some experienced users have experimented with Do It Yourself EQ curves to approximate the RIAA EQ curve imposed on the signal from the record deck by the pre-amp. A Google search for RIAA Curve will produce some useful and highly technical information.

Recording from internal CD drives

Depending on how your computer is configured, Adobe Audition may not be able to receive information from the CD player. Double-click the small speaker icon in the systray (the small area at the bottom right-hand corner of your screen containing the clock amongst other things). The Windows mixer applet will appear. Choose the Options menu. Then choose Properties and recording properties. Press OK. Check that the CD player is enabled and has a small tick in the box next to it. Depending on your sound card you may need to adjust these properties to suit your machine.

Start Adobe Audition, choose Options, Device Order, and check that your sound card is showing properly within the Recording Devices tab. Press F10 and play your sound source, or your CD in the drive. You should see the level meter moving in time with the music. If not, go back check your connections and settings and try again. If your sound card is not showing within the devices tab, you have a hardware problem that needs resolving before you can go any further.

CD ripping

Audio data saved to any CD is stored as data – it's the software inside the CD player that converts the data into sound. Ripping is the practice of extracting audio data as digital information, bypassing the DA converter inside the soundcard. This brings pure digital data into the program, free of any interference. The result can be a purer audio result.

Place an audio CD in the CD drive of your computer and choose File>Extract Audio from CD from the menu bar. The dialog displays each track of the source CD and the track length. Click to select consecutive tracks and either preview to listen or press OK to digitally 'rip' the audio from the CD and import it into the Edit View. Choose 'Time' as the source selection and enter your selection in decimal (00:00:00) form if you prefer. Use the options available if your computer has a new ASPI (Advanced SCSI Programming Interface) or SPTI (on Microsoft NT/XP systems) CD ROM driver. If not, the Generic Win 32 default should suit many older drives and systems. The critical Read Method and Buffer Size options may need to be experimented with until settings suitable for your system are discovered.

Using Adobe Audition to create sound

Although recording from external sources is one way to make noise, Adobe Audition enables the user to create original sounds from scratch using noise or tones, as well as importing audio directly from CD or Quick Time movie. Three sources are used to seed the new waveform; DTMF, Tones and Noise. These are all found under the Generate menu in the Edit View.

DTMF Signals (Generate>DTMF Signals)

DTMF (Dual Tone Multi Frequency) tones are the noises made by your telecommunications device (phone, fax, modem, etc) heard when dialling. The tone is actually two tones; a 'low' tone depending on the horizontal row of buttons and a 'high' tone depending on the vertical row. Tones from 697 to 1633Hz are produced. Adobe Audition also has a DTMF generator. You can test this by entering a phone number and holding the phone receiver to the speakers while the tones are played back. Choose Generate>DTMF Signals to invoke the DTMF Generator. As they come they are a little dry but can be livened up no end by changing the break time value from the default to a much more exciting 2. Try entering a familiar dial string and experimenting with the tone time and break time values. It's even possible to create rhythmic passages using DTMF as the key.

Generate noise

Scientific white, pink or brown noise generator. White noise is a sound containing random amounts of each frequency within the range of the human ear. White noise is full frequency meaning that every frequency within range (usually 20Hz to 20kHz) is present in equal amounts. Pink noise is filtered to reduce the perceived loudness of the higher frequencies by reducing each octave by 6dB. Brown noise is filtered even further to produce noise that has apparently more low frequency content. Noise may be generated to use as a seed for your own waveforms. For natural sounding wind noise or rain pink noise is best.

For example, you are asked to provide the sound of wind in trees for a theatrical production:

1 Choose Generate>Noise to produce 10 seconds or so of low intensity (4) pink noise.
2 Apply the Envelope Transform (Effects>Amplitude>Envelope)and choose the ADSR (Attack Delay Sustain Release) preset.
3 Use the graphic page to shape the rise and fall of the wind by dragging the nodes around the graph. Add more nodes by clicking on the line.
4 Choose Spline Curves to produce a natural curve to the noise.
5 Create an EQ curve with the Graphic EQ (Effects>Filters>Graphic EQ) to emphasise more low frequencies.

Apply long reverb (Effects>Delay Effects>Reverb) to the entire waveform. You may wish to generate a couple of seconds silence for the end of the waveform to create a realistic reverb tail.

Stand back and wait for the audience applause!

Tones (Generate>Tones)

Generate tones of any length, frequency and shape using Generate>Tones (Figure 7.18), e.g., to produce a low frequency 'throb':

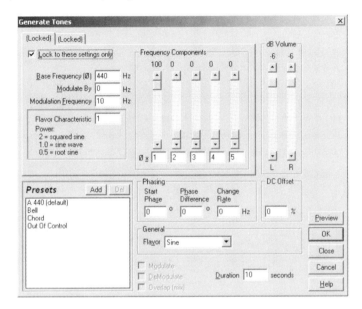

Figure 7.18
Generate tones of any length, frequency and shape

1   Create a new waveform of any length.
2   Choose Generate>Tones and create a 50hz sine wave.
3   Modulate the wave by 20hz with a modulation frequency of 8hz.
4   Choose the first fader and push it to the max. In the general box choose Inv Sine as the flavour.
5   Push 'Preview' to hear the low energy machine throb. To turn this static throb into a landing spaceship push the 2,3,4,5 faders to 59,46,44,76.
6   Remove the check mark from 'Lock to these settings only' and move to the final settings page.
7   On the final settings page make the Base Frequency 20.

Unusual and original samples can be made by modulating noise with tones or the other way around:

1   Generate two or three seconds of any kind of noise.
2   Press Ctrl + A or choose Edit>Select Entire Wave from the menu bar.
3   Choose Generate>Tones and create any tones.
4   Within the dialog enable any of the modulation options to modulate the noise waveform with the tones.

Experiment with different wave shapes and gliding waves to produce creepy space code noises.

Creating original drum sounds from tones and noise

Use the Generate menu to create brand new sounds from the basic building blocks of Tone and Noise. It's extremely easy to create a synthetic 303-style kick drum for instance:

1 Choose File>New and create a empty waveform.
2 Choose Generate>Tones.
3 Create a short gliding sinewave of just .2 seconds starting at 75Hz and ending at just 20Hz.
4 Apply an ADSR curve using the Amplitude>Envelope effect.
5 Apply mild distortion using the Special>Distortion effect. Choose the Distort Bass preset.
6 Apply Dynamics Processing. Choose the Power Drums preset.

The same technique may be used to produce a hi-hat sound:

1 Choose File>New and create a empty waveform.
2 Choose Generate>Noise.
3 Generate a short .1-second burst of white noise with a intensity of 12.
4 Create an envelope with a very short tail using Amplitude>Envelope.
5 Use Filters>Parametric EQ to cut the low and mid frequencies.

The contents of the clipboard may be used to modulate a waveform:

1 Choose File>New and create a empty waveform.
2 Choose Generate>Tones.
3 Generate a 1 second Inverse Sinewave starting at 600Hz gliding down to 20Hz.
4 Choose File>New and create a second waveform
5 Choose Generate>Noise.
6 Generate a 1 second burst of pink noise with intensity of 5.
7 Copy the entire waveform.
8 Use the Window menu to return to the first waveform called Untitled.
9 Mix paste the Pink Noise over the tone using Overlap and a Volume of 8.
10 Apply Sweeping Phaser over the waveform using the Sweep Highs preset.
11 Apply Reverb using the Dark Drum Plate.
12 Apply Dynamics Processing using the TR909 limit preset.

More about modulation

Two sounds may be modulated either by mix pasting from the clipboard or from within the Generate Tones dialog. Modulation happens when the wave data is multiplied by the current tone settings. The result can be bell like sounds or Vocoder effects depending on the target waveform.

Using effects in Edit View

Digital effects may be applied in the Edit View or in the Multitrack View. In the Edit View effects are applied consecutively, that is each effect is in turn affected itself by any effects applied later. In the multitrack view effects can be applied in parallel as if using Auxiliary send and return routing in a conventional mixer. Furthermore effects in Edit View are applied destructively to the waveform. In other words once an effect has been applied and the waveform saved there is no way to remove the effect from the sound. So effects in the Edit View should be seen as tools to sculpt the sound of the waveform rather than to add ambience or other production values.

For instance dynamics processing is a good effect to use over a bass guitar in Edit View as the effect is helping to shape the performance of the guitar player. On the other hand using full reverb on a vocal in edit view may not be such a good idea if the balance for the final mix has not yet been decided on.

Direct X and other effects

Adobe Audition comes with a large number of high quality native effects and is also able to use Direct X effects produced by one of the growing number of third party developers using the original API published by Syntrillium. Most effects have a pre-view function enabling the effect to be auditioned before applying the effect to the waveform. Through the use of third party software called a 'wrapper' it is also possible to use VST effects intended for Cubase as a Direct X effect. Spin Audio have a freeware wrapper that works well for this. Check http://www.spinaudio.com for details of their VST-DX Wrapper. Direct X, VST and native effects may all be used in the multitrack effects racks. TDM effects and plug-ins are not supported.

After installing third party Direct X effects make sure that Effects>Refresh Effects List is selected or the new Direct X effects will not appear in the Direct X list of installed effects.

Native digital effects used in the Edit View only

Adobe Audition has 37 effects types under seven general headings available from the Effects menu. Most of the effects include other effects. E.g. Compression, Expansion and Limiting, etc. are all contained within the simple heading of Dynamics Processing. The effects are:

Amplitude

Amplify (boost or cut volume, apply gliding fades)
Binaural Auto-Panner (stereo only)
Channel Mixer (stereo only)
Dynamics Processing (Compression/Expansion)
Envelope (apply fade in/fade out)
Hard Limiting (mastering tool)
Normalise (set maximum amplitude of waveform)
Pan Expand (stereo only)
Stereo Field Rotate (stereo only)

Delay effects

Chorus
Delay
Dynamic Delay (apply delay over time)
Echo
Echo Chamber (complex echo)
Flanger
Full Reverb (complex reverb)
Multitap Delay
Quickverb
Reverb
Sweeping Phaser

Filters

Dynamic EQ (apply EQ over time)
FFT Filter (very precise EQ)
Graphic Equaliser
Graphic Phase Shifter
Notch Filter (surgically remove specific frequencies)
Parametric Equaliser (most useful EQ)
Quick Filter
Scientific Filters

Noise reduction

Click Pop Eliminator (find and remove clicks and pops from noisy recording)
Clip Restoration (smooths badly clipped recording)
Hiss Reduction (de-essing)
Noise Reduction (analyse and remove noise)

Special

Convolution (waveform takes on character of another from stored impulse)
Distortion (odd distortion tool)
Music (create 'music' by pitch shift and time stretching waveform, stereo only)

Time pitch

Doppler Shifter (very realistic movement simulation)
Pitch Bender (great for special fx)
Stretch (recycle waveform to change pitch or tempo)

Other Effects: Invert, Reverse, Silence

Commonly used basic tools for waveform editing; Invert changes positive numbers into negative ones, effectively turning the waveform upside down. Reverse swaps the waveform end to end for wacky run-out groove messages and Silence transforms a selected range into silence without changing the length of the waveform

Tip

Pure silence in a wave can sound a bit odd. If you have an acoustic guitar piece with many pauses you may consider that silence in the pauses would be a good idea, especially if there is audience noise etc. However pure silence is unnatural (even in space). Instead, copy a few seconds from the beginning or end of the concert and mix paste in the pauses.

The mix paste feature enables data from any of the five clipboards, a file or the Windows Clipboard to be pasted into or over existing data. The data can be repeated (Loop Paste) and crossfaded in which case the current data will fade out while the pasted data is faded in according to values in the Mix Paste dialog. Inserting the data simply moves the existing data to the right and fills the gap with the contents of the clipboard. Overlap places the new data on top of the current data with amplitude decided by the Volume fader. Replace deletes as much existing data as is necessary to accommodate the clipboard data. Modulate modulates the current data with the existing data.

Amplitude and envelope effects

Amplify

The Amplify effect is used to add or remove amplitude power from the waveform, to make it louder or softer in other words. Levels are expressed by either percentage or in DB depending on the presence of a check mark in the dialog. Move the slider to the left to decrease level or to the right to increase level. Values can also be entered manually. If the mouse is clicked over the slider, values can be incremented using the left and right cursor keys. DC Bias Adjust will compensate for a poorly performing sound card by placing the centre of the waveform on the centre

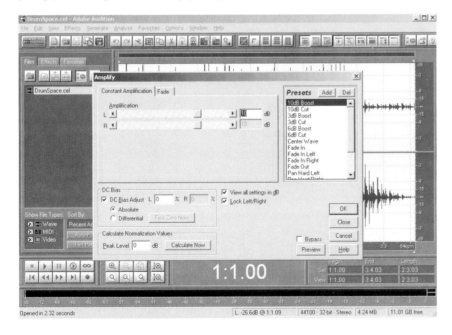

Figure 8.1
Audition's Amplify effect

line. Choose the 'Differential' option to automatically do this or enter a value manually if you want to shift the waveform off centre. Clicking the Fade tab produces two faders. The upper fader is the level of the waveform 'pre-fade' the lower waveform is the level of the 'post fade' wave. Choosing two different values will produce a smooth linear fade over the selected area. Use the Logarithmic option to produce a stronger fade effect.

Binaural Auto Panner

Extremely effective auto-panning tool. Create panning movement along the waveform by dragging handles within the graph to top or bottom.

Channel Mixer

Channel Mixer combines information from both sides of a stereo waveform to create stereo effects such as vocal cut or stereo imaging. Top of the tree for useful things in the list of presets is the Vocal Remover. By inverting the Left and Right channels the information in the centre channel is lost through phase cancellation leaving only the information panned hard left and right at mixdown. Unfortunately this means losing drums and some other parts depending on the recording but the creative possibilities are very exciting. Not available for mono waveforms.

Dynamics Processing

Native Compression and Expansion effects are available from the Dynamics Processing submenu (Effects>Amplitude>Dynamics Processing) (Figure 8.2). The native effects are powerful but as with all things Adobe Audition leans towards the scientific rather than the spectacular for which it's necessary to look at third party Direct X and even VST effects. With this in mind dynamics processing in the digital domain is an incredibly useful and powerful tool. Compression and expansion effects can make the difference between a home recording and a professional sounding product.

Figure 8.2
Native Compression and Expansion effects are available from the Dynamics Processing submenu.

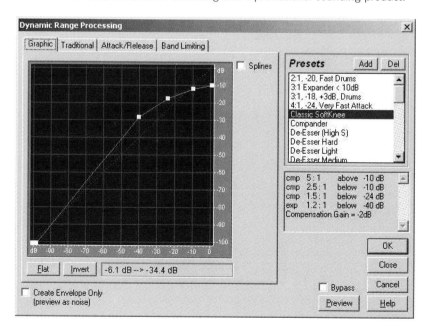

Compression

Compression is most often likened to an automatic finger on the fader of a mixing desk. The compressor attenuates (dips) high amplitude sounds above a preset threshold in order to produce the greatest signal to noise ratio from the program material. In simpler terms the compressor boosts quiet sounds and softens loud sounds in order to make the music easier to listen to. Compression is also used to prevent distortion when mastering by increasing headroom (the margin between maximum amplitude and the point where distortion will happen)

Expansion

Expansion is the opposite to compression. Sounds below the input threshold are attenuated in order to remove background noise for instance. Sounds above the threshold are boosted.

Limiting

A limiter imposes a ceiling at which all sounds are instantly attenuated. Such limiters are often called 'brick wall' compressors as the amplitudes are simply chopped back to the threshold limit rather than being gently attenuated depending on the input level.

Noise gating

Noise gating is a simple type of expansion. Levels below the input threshold are very heavily attenuated. The result is the creation almost of a switch, cutting the sound off when it reaches a certain level. Noise gating can be used as a very simple form of noise reduction (although for much better results use the comprehensive noise reduction effects) but post digital-domain is now much more often used as a retro special effect. Create those cool 1980's 'big drum' sounds using noise gating:

1 Load a suitably retro acoustic tom or kick drum sample
2 Apply some serious reverb – well over the top
3 Apply dynamics processing. Use the Noise Gate at 10dB and feel it in the air tonight!

Overview

The main feature of the Dynamics Processing dialog box is a large graph with input (X, left to right) and output values (Y, up and down) calibrated in dB. The centre line shows a waveform that is untouched as each value in the input axis has the same value on the output axis. Click the mouse over the centre line in the graph to add 'nodes' to the line and drag nodes to the edge of the box to delete. For example, choose the 2:1, -20 Fast Drums preset from the list of presets in the dialog. The graph shows that any information under –20dB will be attenuated gradually by a ration of 2:1 until data with an amplitude of 0db arriving at the input of the compressor at 0db is attenuated to –10db. To compensate for this the output gain is boosted by 6db.

   Use the mouse to click on the line at the point where the input and output values meet at -30db. Drag the new handle left along the green line by two 'squares' until it reaches the –50dB threshold on the input (x) axis. This new line enables expansion to be applied below a threshold of –50dB and compression to be applied below a threshold of –20db. Parts of the waveform arriving at the input of Dynamics Processing with amplitude of –50dB would be boosted by 20dB to –30dB. Below –50dB amplitudes are gradually attenuated to increase the signal to noise ratio. This means that quiet passages of music between –20db and –30db will be amplified slightly according to the input level while amplitudes under –50dB will quietly be attenuated.

This curve will amplify very quiet sounds in the waveform, leaving louder sounds unchanged. On speech this would aid clarity but increase background noise. Over an orchestra recorded in a quiet room this curve would enhance tiny sounds (such as a whispering audience or a soft passage) giving the impression of more detail or even a better recording. To manually enter threshold and ratio values use the 'traditional' tab or right click on any node within the graphics page to see the details for that section. Use the 'splines' option to produce subtle 'soft knee' compression effects that are very suitable for vocals. The Dynamics Processor includes powerful tools for Gain Processing and Level Detection, etc. but does not include any sidechain. Sidechaining in Adobe Audition (using the amplitude of one instrument to control the amplitude of another) is performed using a multitrack transform called 'Envelope Follower' and is discussed elsewhere in this book.

Creative use of Dynamics Processing

Because all processing is done in the digital domain, the compression or expansion effect can be tailored to suit a any waveform, like having a different digital multi band compressor for each instrument – or even each note! Dynamics Processing can liven up a dull and lifeless performance, bring new life to an archived recording, or add missing feel to a rhythm track. For example; you have a stereo drum track recorded using two or three good quality microphones but somehow the snare and kick need emphasis.

- Load the stereo waveform and select a small section of the drummer in full flow. (previewing a four minute wave takes a long time so try the transform on a selection first).
- Choose Effects>Dynamic Processing and flatten the centre line (push the Flat button on the Graphic page).
- Snare drums live in the mid frequency range (200 – 800Hz) so emphasising the snare means boosting only these frequencies. This is called multi-band compression.
- Choose a medium light curve, at the moment the entire frequency range will be affected so the drums will increase in volume.
- Go to the Band Limiting page and enter 200 in the low cutoff and 600 in the high cutoff. Compression is now applied only to the midrange frequencies, including the snare which should now be more apparent.
- Put a check mark in the Create Envelope Only box to hear an amplitude envelope (noise). With a little care you can tune the transform to the shape and frequency of the snare drum.
- Kick drums occupy 75Hz – 150Hz. Use this technique to make the low frequencies punchier although it's a careful balancing act between this and the snare.

This technique is also very useful for enlivening old LP's and tapes before burning to CD. A dull bass part could also be brought to life by identifying the frequencies of the accent notes and emphasising those frequencies accordingly.

Envelope

Envelopes in the Edit View are used to shape the waveform itself. The envelope effect allows the drawing of a envelope curve over the selected area or the entire waveform if no area is selected (Figure 8.3). Click the mouse over the centre line to produce a 'node' that is then pushed into place. To remove a node drag it to the right or left until it either meets another node or the side of the box. To add level to the envelope increase the 'Amplification' value past %100. Checking 'Spline Curves' produces a smooth envelope. This is a very creative effect that can produce dramatic effects.

When creating long fades with the envelopes tool, try to mimic the way that the engineer or producer would use the master fader. Natural fades seem to start almost imperceptibly but tail off steeply towards the end of the fade. A concave bow in the graph produces a fade that will keep the attention of the listener right to the end.

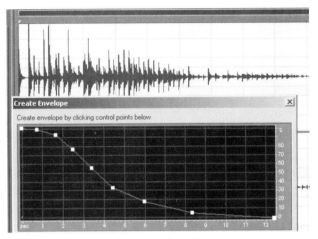

Figure 8.3
The Envelope effect applies the envelope to the waveform as in this fade out effect.

Hard limiting

Hard Limiting is a mastering and mixdown tool for waveforms with a consistent level except for occasional large 'spikes' maybe caused by cymbal crash or other transient sounds (Figure 8.4). Normalising this kind of waveform would not work as normalising detects the loudest part of the waveform only then applies the same calculation over the entire wave. Hard Limiting reduces and softens the level of the 'spikes' while amplifying the rest of the waveform accordingly. If used without care this will totally destroy the dynamics of a musical piece. However it's useful in small doses for mastering live recordings or spoken word.

Hard limiting is very useful for reducing the dynamic range of final mixes, especially Top 40 material intended for radio play or for creating radio advertisements that really spring out at the audience. Use the values in the Hard Limiter dialog to tune the effect to suit your material. Limiting the max amplitude to .5db maximises the amplitude of the waveform to just under the point where it would clip. Raising the input gain lowers the dynamic range. The Statistics function shows what percentage of the waveform would clip if hard limiting were not applied.

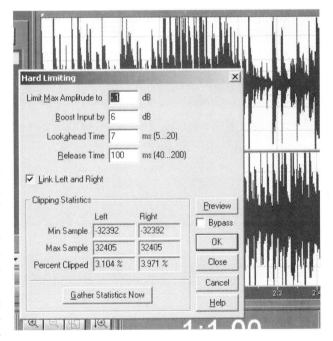

Figure 8.4
Hard Limiting enables the dynamic range of the waveform to be compressed as far as possible.

Normalize

Normalising is used to raise the overall level of the whole waveform (or the selected area) as far as possible to the point where clipping will happen (0dB). The amount by which the entire waveform (or section) is amplified depends on the maximum values within the waveform. So a waveform with a single peak of –3dB would receive an overall boost of 3dB (if normalising was set to %100). A waveform with a large dynamic range, such as a percussion solo, will not benefit much from normalising. For instance a snare roll peaking at –2dB will only produce a 2dB boost – not much good if your soft triangle part is at –20dB. Use the Normalise effect 'pre-production' to boost a low amplitude waveform bearing in mind that any noise will also be normalised at the same time. For details of how to use normalise as a mastering aid see 'RMS Normalising of CD compilation in preparation for burning'.

Pan and Expand

If the Pan / Expand transform is applied to a musical piece, the effect is very mild. However on a spoken word soundtrack or radio production the effect is more pronounced and produces realistic '3D' imaging from a conventional stereo waveform. The clearest way to examine this effect is to generate a stereo waveform containing a few seconds of white noise generated using the 'Spatial Stereo' option. This option produces two channels of white noise delayed by whatever value is appropriate, usually around 500ms. Apply the pan expand effect over the white noise to hear Adobe Audition split the noise into low and high frequency bands then pan the bands to alternate sides of the stereo image.

Stereo Field Rotate

Produces moving pan effects when applied to a stereo waveform. The effects are subtle but great for adding the illusion of movement to a soundtrack, two people having a conversation while walking down a hallway for instance. Creating movement is very simple. The graph plots time against degrees. To create a simple pan for instance all that is necessary is to draw a line that bisects the graph top left to bottom right. If necessary a more complex graph can be created and made to loop over the selected range.

Delay effects

Native delay effects include the usual Reverb and Delays etc. as well as some 'special' effects such as the impressive Sweeping Phaser and Dynamic Echo.

Chorus

Traditional chorus effect produced by splitting the input and delaying one half slightly. The Adobe Audition effect includes all the features found in hardware effects. The use of the chorus effect is fairly straightforward and the developers have obviously had some fun creating the presets. The best way to get a hold of the chorus effect is simply to load a few presets and see what is possible. Binaural cues should only be used when your mix is to be played on headphones only as the effect can sound off balance through speakers.

Delay

Not to be confused with Echo. Delay introduces small amounts of delay into each or both of the stereo channels up to a maximum of 500ms. The presets explore this effect very thoroughly with effects from slapback tape echo to Elvis impressions! The vocal presence presets can produce great results on poorly recorded vocals.

Dynamic Delay

Dynamic Delay introduces the ability to produce flanging and chorus effects that don't require a fixed modulation frequency. In other words; the effect can be dramatic over the first second of a waveform but dying away over the following seconds. This isn't possible in any other way without either re-recording through external hardware or by the use of several presets applied consecutively. To demonstrate these effects generate 10 seconds of white noise. Then choose Effects>Delay Effects>Dynamic Delay to invoke the effects dialog.

The dialog box (Figure 8.5) contains two graphs. The upper graph dictates the

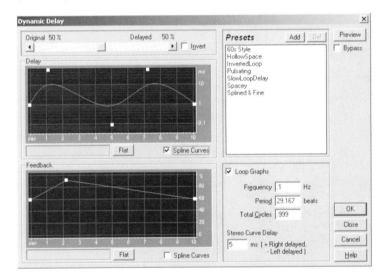

Figure 8.5
Dynamic Delay allows for moving delay effects.

amount of time (up to 50ms) by which the dry signal will be delayed. The lower graph dictates the amount of feedback that will be introduced to the delayed sound. The X axis of the graph indicates time. This axis shows either the entire waveform or just the selection, depending on your decision. For this example I've used 10 seconds of white noise in order to clearly hear the effect. Click on the line in the upper graph to create a new node. Check the option to spline curves and push the button called 'flat' to reset the graph. Drag this new node to the upper edge of the graph at 1 sec 44 ms. Note the status field just under the graph indicates the values under the cursor. Create another node at 5 secs 0.1 ms, and finally a third at 7secs 46 ms. The centre line is at 1ms. Press the preview button to hear the flanging effect.

In the lower graph create one node with a value of 80% at 2 seconds. Press preview again to hear the flanging effect again. Notice how the effect is more pronounced over the first five seconds as the feedback intensifies this portion of the wave. This deliberately simple example uses a regular frequency but of course the

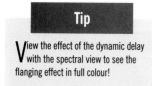

Tip

View the effect of the dynamic delay with the spectral view to see the flanging effect in full colour!

real value of this effect is the ability to produce effects which can be tailored to suit the waveform. Imagine a heavy metal guitar solo in which the performer is using the tremolo arm with irregular frequency. Wouldn't it be great to apply the flanging effect exactly in time with each movement of the arm?

An irregular waveform can be made to loop in regular intervals by checking the Loop Graphs checkbox. Notice the X axis changes to represent the value in the Period field. The flanging effect will now loop at this frequency over the waveform. Changing the values in any one of the Loop Graph fields will cause the program to calculate new values for the other fields.

Echo

Analogue and digital echo devices have been around for as long as tape recorders. The Adobe Audition Echo effect introduces the ability to attenuate frequencies within the echo repeats to produce interesting 'lo-fi' echo effects. As with each of the effects the presets are the best place to start experimenting. Enable 'Continue Echo Beyond Selection' to create repeats that extend beyond the selected area.

Echo Chamber

The Echo Chamber effect is more complex than the plain Echo effect as it enables the specification of room sizes and characteristics in order to simulate (as far as the effect is able to) actual listening environments. The difficulty with this effect is that the interface requires numeric values to be calculated or measured for the required environment but it is remarkably effective. This effect is particularly good for spoken word (or dialogue). The effect is too complex for a musical piece although spectacular special effects can be produced with this effect; the opportunity to put vocalists in a long wooden coffin is probably only something that certain gun owning '60's record producers have had access to until now! This effect requires more processing than simpler effects and preview isn't immediate, be patient if previewing large range selections. See the help file for detailed descriptions of each parameter.

Flanger

Flanging creates the classic 'Jet Plane' effect typical of nearly any record from the late Sixties and early Seventies. Editing presets to create new sounds is as easy as moving the slider bars or even entering new numeric values directly. The rate and frequency values are entered as numbers. Enter a new number in the Period box within the Flanger dialog to adjust the rate of the flanging effect. For slower rates enter larger numbers. Values between .1 and 3 second are most useful. Numbers to 12 decimal places are acceptable. Edit the values in the Flanger effect dialog box to produce a dramatic 'Jet Plane' effect:

Original-delayed	97%	**Rate**	
Initial Mix Delay	1.73ms	Frequency	.166Hz
Final Mix Delay	0ms	Period	6.024s
Stereo Phasing	180 deg	Total Cycles	1.267
Feedback	79.3ms		

The Stereo Phasing option is only enabled over a stereo waveform. Adjust the Feedback and Mix sliders to suit the program.

Full Reverb

The Full Reverb effect is the most complex reverb and the most natural sounding. Full Reverb uses convolution impulses to create the effect and so avoids the introduction of artefacts such as metallic or ringing sounds. This effect is CPU intensive and will slow the rendering of a background mix comprehensively therefore it is recommended that the Full Reverb effect is used mainly within the Edit View.

Use the sliders or enter values in the dialog box to create reverb sounds.

General Reverb

Total Length	Reverb decay
Attack Time	Pre delay or envelope. Essentially how long the reverb will take to reach full effect
Diffusion	High diffusion for smooth reverb or low diffusion for more echo in the reflections
Perception	Builds variations in the effect so as to sound more natural
Set reverb based on early reflection	Automatically creates attack time and total length values for room size set in the next tab

Early Reflections Tab

Room size	The volume of the room in cubic metres
Dimension	The ratio between the width and depth of the room
Source	Simulates the effect of the source being placed to the right or left of the virtual room rather than dead centre
High pass cutoff	Prevents low frequency loss in small room sizes. Use values between 80Hz and 150Hz

Set Reverb Based On Early Reflection, Automatically creates attack time and total length values for room size set in this tab. Duplicate function.

Colouration Tab

Amplitude sliders	Low, mid and migh frequency amplitude
Frequency sliders	Frequencies affected by amplitude sliders
Mid band Q	The width of the mid band frequency range
MS	The decay in ms of each frequency. Recommended settings are between 250 to 700ms

Mixing Section

Original signal	Amount of dry signal present in the mix
Early reflections	Set at about half of the value of the original signal slider for natural reverb
Reverb	Amount of effected signal present in the mix
Include direct	Enhances the result when used with a stereo file over headphones to give a true stereo effect.
Combine source left and right	Combines the input signal to enable faster processing for when mono input source is present.

Preview

Previews the effect before applying over the waveform. Because this is the most complex effect the preview is not available in real time and is recalculated each time a value is adjusted. Adjusting the Mix control or Include Direct Option does not require the preview to be rebuilt.

Multitap Delay

It is possible to chain up to ten echo devices together to create extreme echo effects using this effect. As well as being chained together the devices can be placed inside each other. Each device has independent settings;

Offset	Image is taken from the furthest point and mixed back to an earlier point
Delay	The time in milliseconds between the image and the delayed audio mixed back into the effect
Feedback	The amount of delayed signal to be fed back into the mix. Higher values create extreme amounts of noise

Pressing 'Add New' in the dialog creates another delay device. The current delay device is indicated by a red line in the delay plot while other devices have blue lines.

Allpass feedback	Enable to reduce clipping
Low and high cut filters	Enables filters to be created for each device independently so creating unusual effects such as all bass or all treble delay
Cutoff	The frequency at which the low or hi cut filter will affect the delay
Boost	A negative setting (−1) to attenuate frequencies above or below the threshold
Channels	Enabled when the effect is applied over a stereo waveform enable the effect to be applied individually or to a combination of the stereo channels

Quickverb

A simple reverb, very easy on the CPU and recommended when creating effects racks containing reverbs in the Multitrack View as many more effects can be applied to a session with no impact on performance.

Reverb

Reverb with more parameters. As this reverb is less complex than the full reverb it is more suitable for use in the Multitrack View where one or more Reverb effects can be used within effects racks with very little load on the CPU. It is still a convolution-based effect and so is heavier than many of the other effects.

Sweeping Phaser

Another of those great sixties effects most often used on guitars but essential for manipulating noise when creating original sounds. Like all the other effects the Sweeping Phaser uses numeric values instead of friendly rotary controls. Find a preset closest to the idea you have in mind and edit to taste.

Sweep gain	Boosts the effected sound coming back into the mix. Take care to avoid clipping
Centre frequency	Set to the middle of the slider for best results or to the left and right for bass and treble phasing

Depth	The depth of the effect in Q (ratio of width to frequency)
Resonance	The amount of phase shift applied to the delayed portion of the signal
Sweeping rate	Speed of the effect. Useful as it enables the effect to be set to BPM (although not in sync with the session). Use fractions to set note values; a setting of 240 would produce quavers if the session tempo were 120bpm
Sweep modes	Sinusoidal is the most common or triangular for special effects
Filter type	If low pass option is chosen the effect will not be applied to any frequency below the threshold set by the centre frequency slider
Master Gain	Instead of attempting to balance each of the values to produce a strong effect without clipping the Master Gain value enables the output to be attenuated

Filters and EQ

Filters are incredibly powerful tools for adjusting tone and volume. There is no limit to the way that these tools can be used imaginatively. Use the Parametric Equalizer for simple or complex frequency enhancement. Complex troubleshooting can also be performed using this tool. For example; You have recorded an acoustic guitar but the performer occasionally introduces 'string noise' into the recording. As the string noise is at a constant frequency it is possible to isolate it and soften it using parametric equalization. Select part of the waveform containing the string noise. Choose the preset called 'Reset To Zero' to flatten the curve and clear the bench. Press preview to hear the range selected earlier. The range will repeat until 'Stop' is selected.

Put a checkmark in the centre frequency box 1 and push fader one on the right of the screen until a bell curve appears in the graph. Now move the centre frequency slider from right to left until the string noise becomes much more apparent. You are looking for the range of frequencies that match closely the frequencies in the string noise, probably centring on 6kHz. Depending on the string noise and the quality of the recording it's possible to narrow the width of the centre frequency to pinpoint almost exactly the frequency to be removed, Experiment with values of between 80 to 100.

When the string noise has been identified and boosted dramatically pull fader one down to a negative value (probably between –6 and –10dB) to soften the noise of the string without affecting the natural sound of the guitar. When it's right – press Stop to stop the playback and OK to apply the effect. It's important to perform this operation over just the areas affected by the string noise.

Press the 'Add' button, enter a name for the preset (you can call it anything you like up to a limit of 62 characters eg: '6kHz String Noise remover') and store it for the next opportunity. After a while you'll own a library of instant presets for every job bringing editing time right down and your reputation as a pro, right up. Try doing that with four feet of racked equipment.

Precise editing and shaping of frequencies can be an incredibly creative tool. For instance a very boring drum sample can immediately be livened up simply by accenting one or more kicks or clicks within the sample. The classic 'telephone voice' vocal sound is a simple but highly effective effect (but go easy on it – it's often over used!) for picking out words or phrases within a vocal. Boosting frequencies with High 'Q' values (over 80) produces 'ringing tones', great for robotic vocals and special effects. At the other end of the scale, consistent mains hum (called 60 cycle hum) or noise produced by malfunctioning equipment can be very precisely 'notched out'. Adobe Audition has terrific, leading edge noise reduction tools but the Parametric equaliser is perfect for day to day bench work on difficult waveforms (remove those stubborn stains with new Parametric Equalizer!).

Aside from the parametric equaliser, the second most easily recognisable filter is the Graphic Equaliser. The graphic equaliser allows the creation of EQ 'Curves' which are applied to track length waveforms rather than small ranges or sections. Curves are useful as they enable the engineer to visually choose the desired shape of the frequency curve. However it's a blunt tool compared to the parametric equaliser and is often used for simple bass or treble lifts, etc. For example, you may have a bass guitar track which was recorded badly, leaving nothing in the middle frequencies. Because it was recorded badly there's little mileage in trying to identify the exact frequencies that need boosting. Instead, the engineer may try to simply apply a general curve to the whole bass track in an attempt to 'tune' it to the song and the other instruments. Adobe Audition enables you to add any filter to an effects rack and 'tune' the sound in real time while listening to the other instruments in the multitrack session. The graphic EQ offers 1 Octave (10 bands), ? Octave (20 Band) and 1/3 Octave (30 band) equalisers.

Graphic EQ as a mastering aid

For many people the luxury of a tuned and acoustically perfect mixing environment is something to dream about. The reality is that most EQ tasks are performed in acoustically 'coloured' environments using the best equipment available of course but still suffering from poor speaker placement, reflections and resonant frequencies. Real time analytical software such as Spectrum Analyser Pro (http://www.pas-products.com) can help to discover which frequencies are colouring your listening environment and can produce an EQ curve. This can then be manually applied to the Graphic Equaliser effect and saved as a preset to be applied to your finished mixes. Hitsquad (http://www.hitsquad.com) is good place to start looking for tools like these.

Dynamic EQ

Dynamic EQ enables the gradual cut or boost of any frequency range over time. This effect can be used to produce 'bass kill' or 'treble kill' effects in dance music, Wah-Wah effects for guitars and many other creative effects. The effect is only enabled over a stereo waveform. To use this effect on a mono waveform; convert the mono waveform to stereo and if necessary convert back afterwards.

Creating effects using Dynamic EQ

1 Create a waveform containing white noise of 10 seconds duration with an intensity of 12.
2 Invoke the Dynamic EQ dialog (Effects>Filters>Dynamic EQ) (Figure 8.6). The dialog contains three graphs, similar in use to the Dynamic Delay effect. The uppermost graph dictates how much gain is applied over time. To hear this effect work it's necessary to create a graph which will cut 20dB of gain over the last five seconds of the waveform.

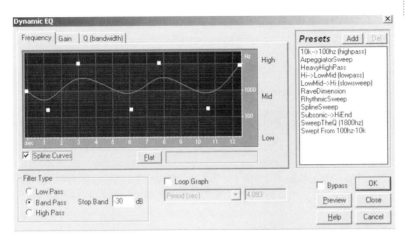

Figure 8.6
The Dynamic EQ dialog.

3 Use the mouse pointer to create a new node by clicking on the blue line in the upper graph.

4 Create a node at 5 seconds and then drag the right handle as far as it can go to the bottom of the graph.

5 Notice how the status bar shows current values under the mouse pointer. The centre graph indicates frequency over time. Create a new node at 5 seconds and drag the right handle as far as possible to the top of the graph. The third graph indicates 'Q'; a ratio of width to constant frequency.

6 Create a new node at 5 seconds and drag the left handle as far as possible down to the bottom of the graph.

7 Press Preview to hear the filter effect as the high frequencies are gradually cut from the waveform until only the frequencies below 1000Hz (the centre line in the Frequency Graph remain.

Creating a Wah-Wah effect

1 Load any suitably rhythmic guitar waveform or record a new part.

2 In the frequency tab move the centre line down to around 150 Hz at both ends (Figure 8.7).

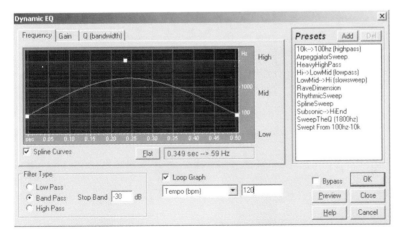

Figure 8.7
Move the centre line down to around 150 Hz at both ends.

3 Create another handle halfway along the line and drag up to around 22050Hz.

4 Ensure Spline Curves is enabled.

5 In the gain tab create another handle half way along the centre line and drag fractionally up to create a boost of about 8db. Again ensure spline curves is enabled.

6 Enable the Loop Graph feature and choose BPM from the drop down box then enter the session tempo.

7 Choose Band Pass in the Filter Type options.

FFT Filter

Use the FFT Filter (Figure 8.8)when presented with an EQ task that involves 'notching out' very small frequency bands, for example when removing air conditioning noise from a recording. FFT filters are also useful when creating band pass filter (which reject frequencies above and below pre-set thresholds), low pass or high pass filters. If you have access to specifications from mixing desk manufacturers or manufacturers of outboard equipment it is possible to build tools to mimic the effect of recording equipment hardware on a waveform. The FFT Filter allows the 'morphing' of one setting into another over time. This produces similar results to the Dynamic EQ tool although doesn't allow for more than one 'morph' whereas each node on the Dynamic EQ graph represents a different state through which the effect will travel over time and these can almost be as many as you like.

Figure 8.8
The FFT filter allows the morphing of one setting into another.

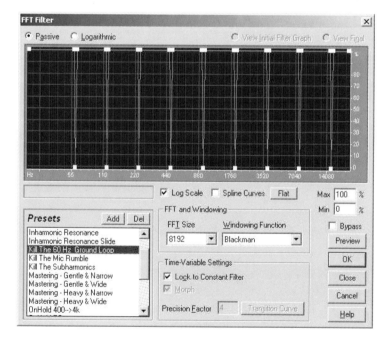

Enable this feature by removing the default checkmark from the 'Lock To Constant Filter' setting. To create target curves or notches choose the 'View Final' option in the top right hand corner of this dialog. Be aware that the preview function does not work when morphing is enabled in this effect. See the comprehensive Adobe Audition Help for detailed instructions regarding this filter.

The notch filter (also available from the Filter menu) offers a very precise method of producing the same results by requiring numeric values from the user rather than presenting a graphical interface. In this way it is possible to surgically remove up to six fixed frequencies without affecting any other frequency above or below. The ability to remove DTMF frequencies in this way is useful when preparing audio for use in radio shows.

Graphic Equalizer

Graphic Equalizers are able to cut or boost frequencies at fixed intervals unlike the parametric equalizer that enables control of frequencies at any interval. The effect is intuitive to use (Figure 8.9). Moving a slider above the centre line boosts the frequency while moving the slider below the centre line cuts the frequency. For general EQ tasks choose the 10 Band (1 octave) or 20 Band (1/2 octave) equalizer. Tasks requiring a finer degree of control use the 30 Band (1/3 Octave) equalizer.

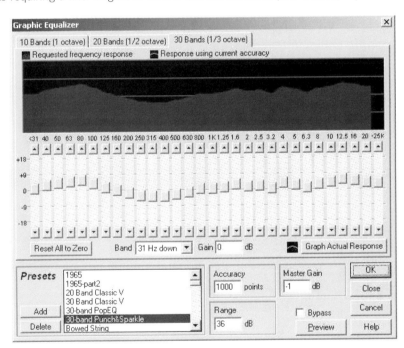

Figure 8.9
Graphic Equalizer.

When equalising low frequencies raise the value of the accuracy control to between 500 and 5000 points. Higher frequencies require less accuracy and therefore less processing time. Lower values in the accuracy dialog reduce the amount of CPU time taken to process this effect. Extend the range of the sliders using the range control between 40 to 180db. This is way beyond the capability of hardware units. Graphic equalisers may be used in the effects racks although for greater control use only 1 or 1/2 octaves and lower accuracy values.

Graphical Phase Shifter

The Graphical Phase Shifter enables phase shifting of any frequency range through 360 deg. Practical applications of this may be correcting phase problems inherited from legacy recordings or removing the effect of phase inversion from a vocal track. Mono to stereo effects can also be produced.

Figure 8.10
The Graphical Phase Shifter.

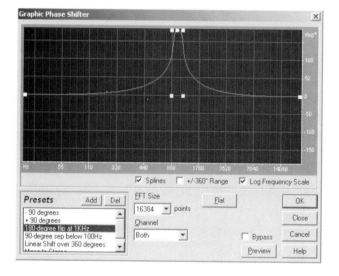

Notch Filter

Notch Filtering enables control of precise frequencies without affecting other neighbouring frequencies. It is used for removing or identifying noise or tones within a waveform. This effect doesn't have much use from a creative point of view although it can be useful when removing artifacts or unwanted noise. Up to six frequencies may be affected in one pass. Enable editing by placing a check mark in one of the 'Tones To Notch' boxes and enter the frequency in Hz. Enter a positive or a negative value in the attenuation box. Choosing Super Narrow from the Width options will only affect the single frequencies specified in the dialog.

Figure 8.11
The Notch Filter can be useful when removing artifacts or unwanted noise.

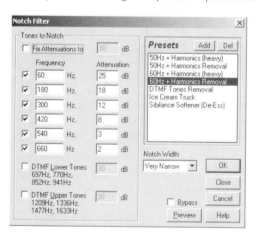

Parametric Equaliser

Parametric EQ requires the user to select a centre frequency and then a width for the frequency range, set ether in 'Q' (ratio of width to frequency) or more uncommonly in Hz. When these values are set the selected frequency range may be adjusted to solve a wide number of EQ problems such as boosting a very broad range of high frequencies or notching out a very slight range of middle frequencies. Parametric EQ is able to handle tasks that Graphic Equalisers cannot, as the Parametric EQ is able to adjust a range of frequencies simultaneously whereas individual sliders on a graphic equaliser must be adjusted individually to achieve a similar result. Up to five frequency bands may be enabled, each may be cut or boosted depending on the source waveform.

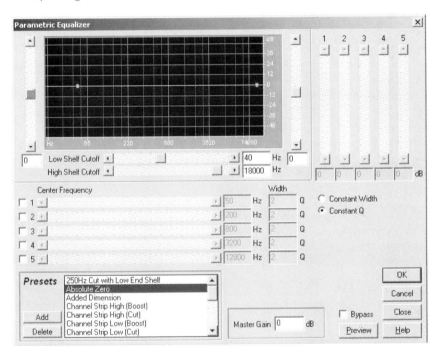

Figure 8.12
Parametric EQ is able to handle tasks that Graphic Equalisers cannot.

Enable a centre frequency by placing a checkmark in any unused box and adjust the slider to the frequency in Hz or enter a value in the dialog manually. Enabling a centre frequency also enables an amplitude slider to the right of the frequency plot. Move the slider up or down to cut or boost frequencies. The range of these sliders is very short so be careful as moving the mouse just a fraction can introduce a cut or boost of many dB. Enter values manually for better control.

Next to each frequency slider is a Width or Q value depending on the option selected in 'Constant Width/Constant Q'. Constant Q is the most common setting. The width of the frequency range being affected is set here. Enter lower values to affect a larger range of frequencies and a larger value to affect a smaller range of frequencies.

On the right and left of the plot are two sliders. The left slider adjusts low shelf amplitude and the right slider adjusts high shelf amplitude. Cutoff values are edited using the sliders below the plot.

Tip

Values adjusted using the X (centre frequency) and Y (amplitude) slider are shown on the plot in real time. Click over the small dots in the lot and drag to new locations for an alternative method of editing.

Quick Filter

Envelope filter like effects can be produced with the 'Quick Filter' transform. This transform enables varying tone control over time (like using the EQ control on a mixer as the track is playing) – instead of a fixed frequency adjustment, or broad EQ curve applied to the waveform as a whole. The effect is subtle over time but the Quick Filter tool is powerful as each fader is a centre frequency for a bell curve so boosting 7.3kHz is pushing frequencies around that centre frequency too. For example to produce a 'Waves on shingle' white noise sound:

Figure 8.13
Quick Filter enables varying tone control over time.

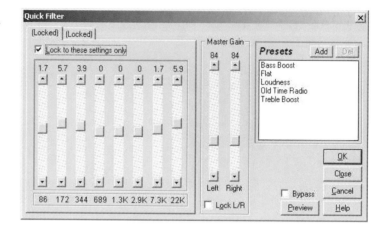

1 Create about 12 seconds of white noise using Generate>Noise.
2 Select the entire waveform and remove the checkmark in 'Lock to these settings only'.
3 On the first page boost 86,172,689, 7.3 and 22k by about 20%.
4 On the Final Settings page drop the same bands by about 30%. You'll hear a bass and treble boost gradually diminishing towards the end of the noise sample.
5 Create 'pulsing' effects using a short white noise sample (.5 secs) and extreme quick filter settings.
6 Insert the wave into the multitrack and duplicate as necessary or simple copy and merge paste into one waveform several times.

Scientific Filters

Adobe Audition also offers high quality Scientific Filters using IIR (Infinite Impulse Response) filters for extremely accurate notch filtering, band pass and low pass filtering (Figure 8.14).

Waveform and Spectral View

Waveform data may be viewed as the default 'Waveform View' and an additional 'Spectral View'. Most times viewing as waveform data is preferable as spectrum data requires significantly more resources leading to a decrease in computer response.

• Waveform view shows amplitude data but not frequency data.
• Spectral View shows both frequency data and amplitude data as colour.

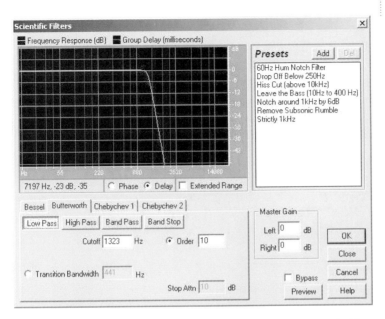

Figure 8.14
Adobe Audition offers high quality Scientific Filters

The effect of filters and EQ on a waveform is easily seen using the Spectral vView (Figure 8.15). Occasional monitoring of the waveform in this way can reveal EQ problems before the waveform is saved. The Spectral View is also essential for identifying the frequency range of tones or noise within a waveform. Swap between Waveform and Spectral Views using the toggle button on the menu bar. Frequency (tone) information is displayed as varying colours inside the waveform instead of

Figure 8.15
The effects of a flanger over pink noise is easy to see in the Spectral View.

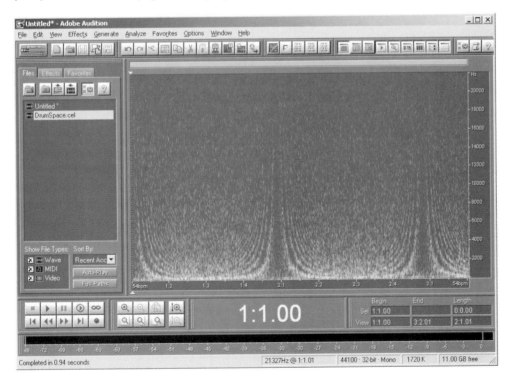

the solid green wave in waveform view. The Amplitude ruler is replaced with a frequency ruler indicating frequencies in hertz from zero at the lower end to 22kHz at the top, depending on the way in which the waveform was recorded.

In this view amplitude is shown as colour intensity from deep colours for low-intensity to very bright colours leading to white for high-intensity. So a waveform rich in bass energy would show bright colours at the lower end of the spectrum towards the ruler line.

Please note that most people can't hear above 12,000Hz, everything from 13,000 to 22,000 is inaudible, except to your dog! However data in this range is still recorded by Adobe Audition 1.0. Mp3 and other 'lossy' compression formats discard data in this region and below about 10 or 20 hertz when encoding raw WAV data.

Tip

Colour Options for Spectral settings are found within Options>Settings. Incidentally, reversing the colours is a toggle. To reverse the colours back to default check 'reverse the colours' again.

Advanced tools and digital effects

Adobe Audition contains all the tools you'll need to create fantastic effects, rivalling and in most cases exceeding the capabilities of external devices. However creating great effects and new sounds are just some of the things that the pro-audio engineer needs to do to keep clients happy. Most waveforms come in with real problems. Noisy recordings are very common or recordings that contain clipped data. In this case you'll be glad you have Adobe Audition noise reduction, widely regarded to be the best in the industry. Some recordings need to be balanced to minimise the effects of too much EQ applied at the mixing desk. Use the Parametric Equalizer and Notch Filter to rescue recordings affected in this way. Some waveforms sound unusable until a few carefully chosen effects and procedures bring them back to life making you into a first call engineer for your client. Away from the studio Adobe Audition is invaluable for restoring and archiving old records, cleaning up radio conversations or simply creating CD compilations for the car.

Click and Pop Eliminator

The Click and Pop Eliminator (Figure 8.16) is an archiving tool created for the easy removal of clicks, pops and scratches from a recording made of an old and damaged vinyl (or any other material) LP. The process is as simple as making a waveform of the source material and choosing Effects>Noise Reduction>Click and Pop Eliminator from the menu bar. Within the dialog box press the Auto Find All Levels button to scan and detect clicks and pops within the waveform. This effect doesn't offer a preview function and the process of scanning the waveform can be lengthy, especially when applied over a long section of audio. For this reason select a typically noisy section to experiment with and when happy with your results save this as a preset (just in case of accidents) before applying the transform over the entire length of the recording. The results are spectacular and when combined with a little multi-band compression can completely rejuvenate an old and abused LP. For best results always convert 16bit files to 32bit before applying the Click and Pop Eliminator. Best practise is to work wholly in the 32bit domain and only downsample to 16bit if mastering to CD or preparing the waveform for distribution.

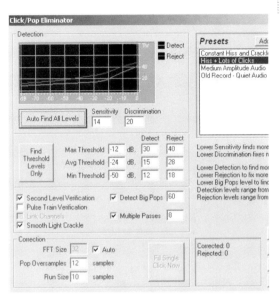

Figure 8.16
Remove clicks, pops and scratches from your recordings with the Click and Pop Eliminator

Clip Restoration

Clipping happens in one of two ways; either as a result of too much level into your sound card from wrongly adjusted external equipment or by over amplification of a waveform. Clipped portions of a waveform are recognisable by being 'chopped off' at the top and bottom and are heard as a distorted sound. If areas of a waveform have become clipped during recording and if the recording cannot be made again such as a live recording it is possible to repair the damaged waveform and reduce the effects of clipping. Convert the file to a 32bit file if not done already and select the entire clipped waveform, including the clipped areas. Apply the Clip Restoration effect with no attenuation then apply the Hard Limiting effect with no boost and a –0.2dB limit.

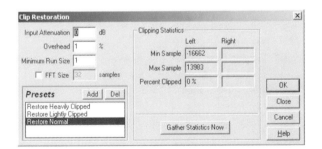

Figure 8.17
Use Clip Restoration to repair damaged waveforms and reduce the effects of clipping

Hiss Reduction

Just as the Pop and Click Eliminator can help when archiving and mastering from vinyl, the Hiss Reduction 'effect' can remove hiss from noisy tape recordings. The results are not as spectacular as with the Click reduction, especially when the music or speech on the tape is only a little more audible than the hiss. But it's still the best tool around for the job. Start as usual by recording the source audio to a 32bit waveform if not done already. Apply the Hiss Reduction tool (Effects>Noise Reduction>Hiss Reduction) to a typically noisy area of the wave and experiment

Figure 8.18
Hiss Reduction can remove hiss from noisy tape recordings.

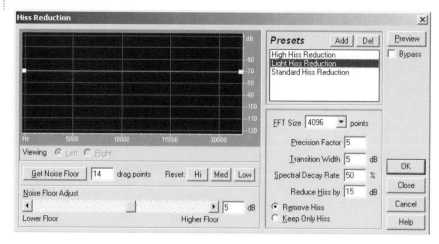

within the dialog to produce the best results. The Hiss Reduction tool is best applied sparingly. An attempt to remove absolutely all evidence of the hiss will result in a 'squelched' sound as portions of the desired information are removed along with the hiss. When selecting audio for analysis before applying the effect try and choose an area of the audio that has no music or speech present and also an area that has a smaller amount of high frequency information. See the comprehensive help files for detailed information on this effect.

Noise Reduction

Use noise reduction any time that the foreground sound is obscured partially by a wide frequency background noise. For example; you have recorded a soft piano piece for an examination but the recording is spoilt by an unnoticed fan heater in the room. The noise is only apparent when you listen back.

Figure 8.19
Noise Reduction.

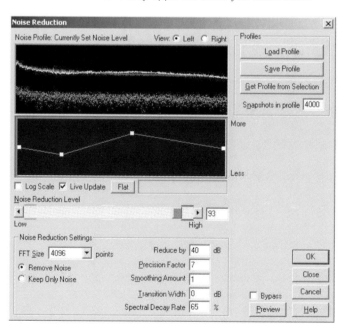

1 If necessary convert the waveform to 32bit.
2 Select any area of the waveform which contains as much of the background noise (in this case the heater) as possible.
3 Choose an area of the containing only the background noise if possible such as the run off at the end of the take.
4 Once a suitably 'noisy' area has been selected choose Effects>Noise Reduction>Noise Reduction from the menu bar (Figure 8.19).
5 Within this dialog choose a Snapshot value of 64 and an FFT Size of 4096. Change the 'Reduce By' value to 40db, the Precision Factor to 7 and the Smoothing Amount to 2.

With these settings in place click on the button 'Get Profile From Selection'. Adobe Audition will scan the selected area and produce a noise profile. The graph now shows detected noise over the frequency range with the low frequencies on the left of the graph. Detected noise appears as tiny yellow dots - one for each frequency (grouped together they appear as a thick yellow line) with the noise floor indicated by green dots.

6 Move the slider bar just below the graph to lessen the amount of noise reduction. As the bar is moved a red line will appear from behind the yellow line to indicate the amount of reduction that will be applied.
7 Preview the effect with different noise reduction levels until the desired result is obtained.

If the noise reduction doesn't appear to be affecting the troublesome frequencies raise the FFT Size to 6000 or more and experiment with other values. When you are satisfied don't press OK! We need to apply Noise Reduction to the entire wave.

8 Press the Close button and return to the waveform.
9 Press Ctrl-A to select the entire waveform and return to Effects>Noise Reduction.
10 The Noise Reduction dialog will open with the previously scanned noise profile still in memory.
11 Press 'Preview' to hear the selection play with the noise reduction profile applied. You should hear a significant drop in background noise.

When completely happy press the OK button to apply the noise reduction effect to the performance.

The noise reduction dialog contains many options for further enhancing the noise reduction effect. The first thing to do is establish whether there is too much noise reduction. Drag the Noise Reduction Level slider from right to left. The Graph at the top of the screen will change to show a red line where the current selection is and a yellow line illustrating the noise reduction. Maximum noise reduction can easily disturb parts of the wave that you want to keep. Experiment with values around 90% or less to retain as much of the musical quality of the piece as possible. Use the 'Keep Only Noise' option to establish how much of the foreground noise is missing. FFT (Fast Fourier Transform) Size determines the resolution (in frequency bands) of the transform. Experiment with values from 4096 to 12000 depending on the nature of the material and the intensity of the background noise.

If the noise profile is louder in certain frequency ranges use the reduction graph to lessen the effect of the noise profile in the un-affected frequency ranges. If the fan heater is on a wooden floor it may produce unwanted noise only in the frequency range 100 – 200 Hz. To apply noise reduction in this range only click on the reduction graph to create a node and drag the node on the extreme right to the bottom of the graph. This lessens the effect of the noise reduction profile in the upper frequencies.

Special effects

Convolution

Convolution is the tool to use when you don't happen to have the cash to hire St Pauls cathedral for your Xmas Choir or if you'd enjoy hearing a rock guitar solo in the British Library. Convolution is also the technique employed to produce stunningly realistic 'modeller' amps and effects. It works because if the samples in one waveform are multiplied with the samples in another the target waveform will adopt the characteristics of the source. In practice this means that an impulse file of a reverberating space (such as the inside of a lift or a huge cathedral) can be imposed on a suitable sound. The effect is to place the sound inside the reverberating space. Literally, using this technique it is possible to put your lead vocalist in La Scala. More realistically convolution is the way to apply the sound of that all important mike or reverb to a waveform. In other words your guitar or vocal can appear to have been treated with the most impossibly expensive reverb or recorded with the best microphones. Of course it's not as easy as all that. Convolution needs two waveforms; the source (your original recording) and the impulse (the sound of the effect). Finding impulse files can be tricky and most people make up their own. But if you can beg or borrow some equipment for a day or so, it's easy to make your own.

A basic impulse file may be created as follows:

1 Close all waves (and sessions if using Adobe Audition 1.0).
2 Choose Generate>Silence from the menu bar.
3 Generate 5 seconds of silence.
4 At the New Waveform dialog choose 44100, mono, 32bit file.
5 Using the Zoom selection tool zoom right into the very start of the new waveform until the individual samples appear as small squares.
6 Double click on the first one and enter 32000 as a value.
7 Return to view the whole waveform.
8 Apply a reverb effect over the whole wave (choose a full, smooth reverb with a long tail in this instance).
9 Drag Select over the reverb impulse taking care to include the whole of the tail.
10 Choose Effects>Special>Convolution.
11 Press 'Clear'.
12 Enter the following values; Scaled By: 1. Volume: 100%.
13 Press 'Add Sel'.
14 Press 'Save' to save impulse in your data partition.
15 Press 'Close'.

Applying your impulse:

1 Load any waveform.
2 Choose Effect>Special>Convolution.
3 Load your saved impulse (if not already loaded).
4 Press OK.

Tip

Convolution may be used to apply a Reverb, EQ and Delay set over a waveform. Apply the effects in turn to the test impulse and save.

At first you'll find that the effect sounds not as expected. Experiment with differing values and reverbs etc. Also try experimenting with filters and delay. Most dynamic effects (Compression, distortion etc.) don't suit convolution.

(Many thanks to 'Drowz72' for permission to use his method of producing an impulse file originally posted to the Syntrillium forum at Audioforums.com in this chapter).

Third party impulse files

More and more third parties are making tools to create impulses. One of the first is Aurora. (http://www.ramsete.com/aurora) Download Aurora's shareware set of xfm (filters) for Adobe Audition as they'll work perfectly with the new Adobe Audition. Unpack the zip file and copy the .xfm files to the directory containing Adobe Audition (c:\program files\Adobe\Audition 1.0). When you start Adobe Audition a new sub-menu called Aurora will have appeared in the effects menu. This contains the filters and tools necessary to copy and effect existing wave files into impulses.

For example: You have a vocal phrase which you'd like to put into a very large room. Create a new 16 bit waveform of same length as the vocal phrase. Generate 0.1 seconds of high intensity (30) mono white noise. Move to the extreme right of the white noise and generate about 10 seconds of silence. Drag select over the white noise and a few seconds of silence and apply a reverb effect. It's important to include some silence or the reverb won't have a 'tail'. The reverb created will be a bit lifeless so apply some low frequencies with the parametric equaliser and smooth the tail with dynamic processing. Copy the reverb waveform to the clipboard.

Return to the vocal phrase and choose Effect>Aurora>Convolve With Clipboard. The Aurora effect will meld the reverb tail and the vocal phrase together. Obviously Reverb is a native effect so this example isn't that useful in practise. But substitute a microphone and speaker in a beautiful room in place of the native reverb and the technique is the same.

Distortion

Don't be tempted to see the Distortion effect as a substitute for your Turbo Rat or Big Muff guitar effects pedal. This distortion is much better used as a 'grungeliser' to mess up your waveforms in the sickest way possible. It does contain some interesting features such as the interesting ability to apply separate distortion values for positive numbers (above the green centre line in waveform view) and negative numbers (below the green line). Simply uncheck the 'symmetrical' box in the Distortion effects dialog to choose this option. The Distortion effect is also great when producing 'lo-fi' sounds or creating retro mixes.

Figure 8.20
Use the Distortion effect as a 'grungeliser'.

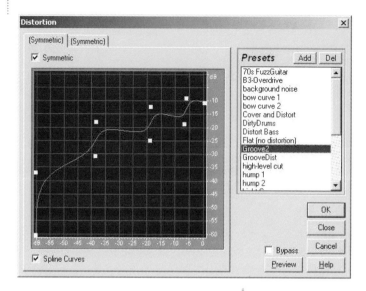

1   Load your mix.
2   Apply a –25db 'brickwall' limiter.
3   Apply the Bow Curve 1 distortion effect.

Music

Any short vocal or musical 'hit' can be turned into something approximating a musical piece. This works best on short samples without pitch. For example a single wood block sample may be turned into a solo piece for marimba. Depending on the placing of musical notes in the Music effect staff, the program will create new instances of the wave 'hit' calculating pitch and duration of each instance and space between them. If you want to do something really odd to a vocal track it's possible to use the Music effect as a 'step time' pitch bender.

1   Generate 0.5 seconds of a tone (440hz will do).
2   Edit Select All or Ctrl + A to select the whole wave.
3   Choose Effects>Special>Music.
4   Drag notes down onto the stave. The notes will simply fall into line as there are no bar lines (Figure 8.21). Drag a note off the stave to remove it.

Figure 8.21
The Music effect

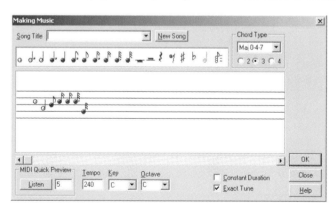

Pressing the preview button generates a musical preview of the arrangement via MIDI. Tempo, key and other values may also be adjusted to suit. The contents of the current clipboard are used by the Music effect as quarter notes. Therefore it's necessary to carefully select the right amount of data as the composition will use the length of the data for timekeeping.

Time and pitch effects

Doppler Shifter

Use the Doppler Shift effect whenever you need to simulate a car or plane passing by. The effect will work on both mono and stereo waveforms although the effect is much more apparent with stereo waveforms. Briefly the Doppler Effect occurs as waves of moving air reach the ear with more or less frequency depending on whether the source (car or train, etc.) is moving towards you, or away from you. The effect is an ascending or descending shift in pitch. The effect combines pitch shift with panning to create the illusion of movement. To illustrate this we can create the noise of a jet fighter passing low overhead at an air show.

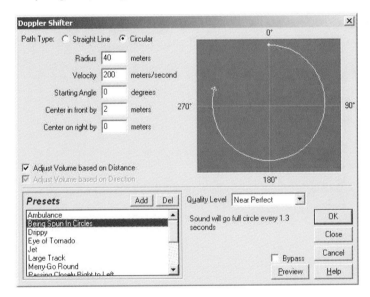

Figure 8.22
Use the Doppler Shift effect whenever you need to simulate a car or plane passing by.

1   Create a stereo 32bit waveform containing 10 seconds of pink noise.
2   Use the Dynamic Delay to create the illusion of screaming engine noise by creating a diagonal line from left to right with values of 0.50ms at the left and 4ms at the right.
3   Use the Doppler Shifter to create a dramatic illusion of movement using the following values; Starting Distance Away: 1500, Velocity:355, Coming From:270, Passes In Front: 75, Passes On Right: 0.
4   Finally press the Preview button and get ready to duck!

Pitch Bender

Does exactly what it says on the tin; calculates how to bend a waveform or range up or down over time and allows previewing, Great for special effects although I've yet to find a musical use for this effect. It's the tool for producing effective

Figure 8.23
Pitch Bender is the tool for producing effective 'turntable power down' and scratching effects.

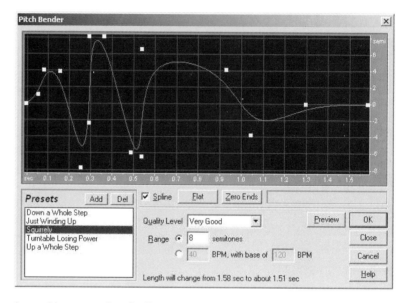

'turntable power down' effects and scratching effects. The most dramatic effects from this effect come from experimenting with the Range values, particularly selecting the BPM option and using values of 90BPM over a base of around 50BPM.

The graphical screen (Figure 8.23) is very useful; as usual enter nodes by placing your mouse over the graph and clicking with the primary (left) button. Drag nodes from left to right or off the screen entirely. Right click over any node to see the value. To create the illusion that your recording is of a multitrack tape select the first second of the recording and create two nodes at the very left hand side of the graph with the following values:

	Time Index	Pitch
Node1	0	6.11
Node2	0.01	7.06

The remainder of the graph should be completely flat. This very small pitch change gives the impression of the reel of tape snatching up to speed, characteristic of the behaviour of a multitrack tape.

The range control in this dialog enables the Y axis to display either semitones or BPM (Beats Per Minute). To raise or lower the BPM of a breakbeat or loop:

1 Load the waveform containing the loop and choose Effects>Time/Pitch>Pitch Bender.
2 Ensure the graph is 'flat' and select the BPM range option.
3 Replace the default value in the BPM range field with 100 BPM and if possible

enter the original tempo of the loop into the 'base of' field although this isn't entirely necessary and won't affect the result. However if your target tempo is critical this value will need to be entered correctly to enable the program to calculate the desired tempo.

4 Right click on the first and last nodes in the graph to manually enter a target tempo.

The Pitch Shifter effect can only change tempo by raising or lowering pitch, it is unable to 'recycle' or change tempo without affecting the sound of the instruments.

Stretch

The Time Stretch effect creates 'Recycle' style accurate pitch shifting for correcting bum notes or bringing drum loops into time. Waveforms may be shifted in pitch, in time without affecting pitch or resampled in which case both time and pitch is affected. The depth of the pitch effect or the speed of the effect is both adjusted by the large horizontal slider bar in the middle of the dialog. Move the bar to the left to slow tempo or to the right to speed up. Confusingly moving the bar to the left raises the pitch while moving it to the right lowers pitch.

Info

When using the Time Stretch effect always enter 100 in the Ratio box as a default value. This value is not the starting BPM of the loop, it is the ratio by which the sample will be stretched. A value of 100 means 'no change', lower or higher numbers mean the sample will be stretched or shrunk appropriately.

In cases where a whole track must be adjusted (perhaps the guitar player was out of time or the singer requires a different key) experiment with chopping the waveform into smaller more manageable pieces in order to perform the task.

It is possible to permanently change the tempo of a loop in BPM using the Pitch Shifter effect after calculating the original BPM of the loop using Edit>Edit Tempo. The pitch (sound) of the loop at the new tempo can then be raised or lowered in pitch using the Stretch tool to preserve the new tempo.

To varispeed bum notes or phrases choose 'Pitch Shift' to keep the crucial timing intact. The Transpose drop down box provides almost an octave of preset transpositions from 11b (flat) to 11# (sharp) these values have no effect when the 'Preserve Pitch' option is chosen. The third option 'Resample' changes both pitch and length depending on the ratio chosen. Choose the Low Precision option in Multitrack View and while previewing. In Edit View choose High Precision (which takes much longer) while applying the effect when you are happy that everything is going to be OK.

Advanced users may choose to apply particular values in the Splicing Frequency and Overlapping boxes. If you aren't sure about the values (and don't have a couple of days to experiment) put a check mark in the 'Choose Appropriate Defaults' box to allow the program to make a fairly accurate (better than mine anyway) guess. The second page of the Stretch effect dialog enables the Stretch effect to produce gliding Pitch Bender style effects (Figure 8.24).

Figure 8.24
The Stretch effect produces gliding Pitch
Bender style effects.

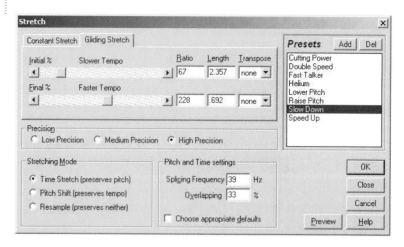

Tip

Pressing F2 on the keyboard re-
applies the last used effect with
the same parameters. This can be
useful when applying an effect over
portions of a waveform without
revisiting the effects dialog or the need
to create a new item in the favourites
menu.

Other 'workshop' features for converting and editing waveforms in the Edit View

Effects are only some of the tools available within the Edit View. The Edit View is also needed whenever waveforms require resampling or converting or when you need to run a script over many files.

Sample rate and sample types, converting

Sample rate is the speed in samples per second at which Adobe Audition reproduces or plays individual samples. The rate of reproduction is so fast that it must be expressed in terms of Hz (thousands of times per second). For instance a sample rate of 44100Hz means 'forty four thousand, one hundred samples will be processed in every second'. When the sample rate is adjusted the audio created from data in the waveform will appear to change pitch. For instance if a waveform created using samples recorded at 44100Hz is made to play back at half the speed (22050Hz) we'll hear that playing back at half the pitch of the original. In other words it will sound 'slowed down'. Choose Edit>Adjust Sample Rate from the menu bar to temporarily adjust the playback sample rate of a wave.

Convert Sample Type

Different programs and technologies require waveforms saved with differing properties. Use Convert Sample Type to render the waveform within Adobe Audition for the target application. Or you may use it to upsample (resample) a low resolution waveform into a higher one. This dialog enables the conversion of any sample to a different sample rate and bit depth. This conversion is permanent once the file is saved. For example; It's good practise to edit waveforms internally with a bit rate of 32bits. This allows for much finer shaping of transforms etc. However, a CD cannot be made from a 32bit WAV file as the CD standard is stuck at 44100Hz and 16bits. To convert a 32 bit file into a 16 bit file suitable for CD:

1 Choose Edit>Convert Sample Type (Figure 8.25).
2 Choose 44100Hz as the Sample Rate and 16 Bit as the resolution.
3 From the Dither box make sure that Enable Dithering is checked and use a value of 0.7 for Dither Depth.

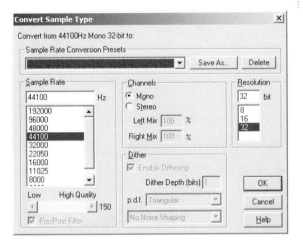

Figure 8.25
Use Convert Sample Type to render the waveform within Adobe Audition for the target application.

4 Choose 'Triangular' in the p.d.f drop down and Noise Shaping 44.1kHz.

5 Finally set the 'Low/High quality' slider to about 800. Choosing high quality takes much more processing time but is preferable to the inferior results produced by low quality.

6 Save these settings by choosing 'Save As', entering 'CD Quality' in the dialog and pressing OK.

This preset will now be available for sessions in the future. Use Convert Sample Type to change a stereo sample to mono and vice versa. The science and mathematics of sample conversion is a subject way beyond the scope of this book. Use the help files if you'd like to know more. Remember that when converting audio from one type to another the results greatly depend on the nature of the data, particularly the range of frequencies that are contained. If the results obtained from these suggestions are not what you expect, experiment with the dither values and noise shaping options until you are satisfied.

Basic audio data concepts

Analogue voltage arriving at the sound card from microphone or keyboard is 'sampled' so many times per second, depending on the capabilities of your sound card. Sample rates can be as low as 8000 (eight thousand times per second) or a as high as 96kHz (ninety six thousand times per second). Adobe Audition is able to record at 10 MHz (ten million times per second) well beyond the specifications of an ordinary sound card. All of these samples would be almost useless without some way of recording how loud the sample should be on playback. The amplitude information is recorded in the 'bit depth'. Music CD's have a bit depth of just 16 bits. In other words a 32bit sample is able to remember twice as many 'steps' as a 16bit sample. The larger the number of steps the better the dynamic range of the waveform. When a 32bit sample is converted down to a 16bit sample the data must be 'dithered' to mask the loss of quality and audio artifacts that appear. To do this the software introduces tiny amounts of noise into the data. The amount of noise, the frequency of the noise and the areas that the noise is introduced into are options available from the Convert Sample Type dialog. It's similar to Adobe Photoshop reducing an artwork that has 650000 colours to one with only 256. Some of the colour information will have to be lost and so it's just a question of making sure that the difference is as little as possible.

To see the sample rate and bit depth specifications for your sound card choose
Options>Settings>Device Properties (or press F4). The range of options for your sound card (or
cards) is shown within the Options dialog box. Many sound cards are able to support recording and
playback up to 96k at 24bit. Professional sound cards all have this specification.

Batch File Convert

Batch processing enables you to open a group of files and convert them all to the same sample rate, bit depth and number of channels (one for mono, two for stereo). After conversion the files may be saved in any format and to any destination. The procedure is as simple as following the steps in the dialog box.

1 Choose File> Batch File Convert
2 In the first tab choose the file or files for conversion
3 In the second tab choose whether the files need to be converted to a different sample rate and bit depth or for conversion from stereo to mono. This is the same tool found in Edit>Convert Sample Type. It is not necessary to convert all files, only if the target format demands it.
4 Choose an alternative target file format if necessary, for example when converting WAV to MP3.
5 Finally choose options for the target. This dialog contains several options. Choose to overwrite existing files if the target folder contains files from earlier conversions or you will be prompted for each file with the same name. Choose to delete the source file if you are confident that the procedure will produce the results you expect. This operation cannot be undone so it is probably better to leave this option unchecked. Choose to remove files from the source list if you have a number of folders to work through.

Delete Silence

Adobe Audition is very often used for the preparation of radio productions and adverts where literally, time is money. It's difficult for voice-over artists to clearly pronounce words extremely quickly but on the other hand silence is dead air – no matter how short. The Delete Silence feature will scan for areas of the waveform with very little or no audio information. It will then automatically delete the silence. This is very effective for creating short, snappy adverts and productions. The transform is intuitive to use. Highlight a range, choose Edit>Delete Silence and push Scan For Silence Now. Adobe Audition scans the waveform and reports back on how much silence was found. If this is too much or too little, edit the values in the

Figure 8.26
The Delete Silence feature will scan for areas
of the waveform with very little or no audio
information and then automatically delete
the silence.

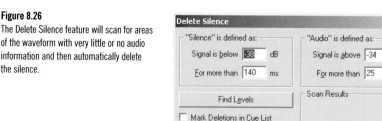

dialog and try again. To make this easier use the Find Levels button which will cause the software to scan the waveform looking for minimum and maximum values.

Zero crossings

A noticeable 'click' is produced if a wave is cut at any other point other than at the centre line. Usually this isn't a noticeable problem as Adobe Audition automatically smoothes the ends of a waveform during recordings or Splice, Cut/Delete, Trim, Adjust Boundaries, drag-copy, and drag-clone. To see this working bring up any waveform and zoom in until the individual samples are visible as small squares along the wave. The area between each square is an individual sample. Choose an area of the visible wave ending between two peaks, drag and select (Figure 8.27). Notice how the range begins and ends away from the centre line. When the range is deleted Adobe Audition smoothes and joins the two ends of the remaining sections together.

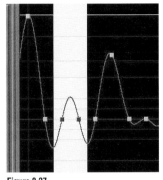

Figure 8.27
A range is selected away from the centre line.

When creating loops etc, it's possible to select a range that begins or ends badly away from the centre line. In this case, Edit>Zero Crossings can be used to find the next place along the waveform at which the wave bisects the centre line. This is useful when selecting loops. For example: You have a bass part which contains a useful phrase. You want the whole phrase but you don't know exactly where the phrase ends, so you can't drag select. The phrase is too complex to manually add markers.

1 Drag select over the phrase in the waveform and zoom to selection so that the entire phrase is visible with a short head and end section for comfort.
2 Choose Edit>Zero Crossings>Adjust Selection Inward to move the selected range inward to the point where the centre line is bisected at both ends.
3 Because the centre line indicates no data or silence, the phrase should naturally fall between these two points.
4 Use the other Zero Crossing options to adjust the selected range at either end. Then press F8 to add this range to the Cue List if required.

Snapping

The playback cursor will snap to the nearest cue marker or ruler calibration depending on options chosen in Edit>Snapping. Because the ruler is unlikely to line up with critical areas in the waveform it's more useful to choose snap to cues. In this way cue markers can be defined first then the playback cursor will snap to each cue making working through the waveform much easier. In Multitrack View three more options are added to the snapping list:

Snap to Blocks	Waveblocks will 'snap' against each other. Useful when moving loops etc.
Snap to Loop Endpoints	Snaps to the end of a looped waveform
Snap to Frames (Always)	Used when Time Display Format is set to any of the SMPTE frames options. Snaps only to whole frames and not to ruler calibrations

Edit Tempo

Through analysing the waveform Adobe Audition can get a good idea of the tempo of a sample (especially drum samples) and use this tempo for the session. This works best on fairly simple drum samples without too much ride or background percussion as it analyses peak amplitudes and the distance between them. So background noise, particularly on a heavily compressed sample will reduce the accuracy of this feature.

Extracting the tempo from a drum sample

1 Load a drum sample waveform and press Ctl – A to select the whole sample.
2 Place the playback cursor at the beginning of the first beat in the waveform (using a kick drum).
3 Play back from your marker and find the end of the first bar.
4 Drag select over the first marker past the end of the bar.
5 Use the range adjust keys (H,J,K and L on the keyboard to adjust the range of the selection until the looped area makes musical sense and feels right. Loop if necessary.
6 Right Click in the Time Display field and choose Edit Tempo from the menu (Figure 8.27).
7 In the Extract From Selection section replace the value in the Beats Highlighted field with the correct number of beats in your selection.
8 Push the extract button to extract the tempo from the sample

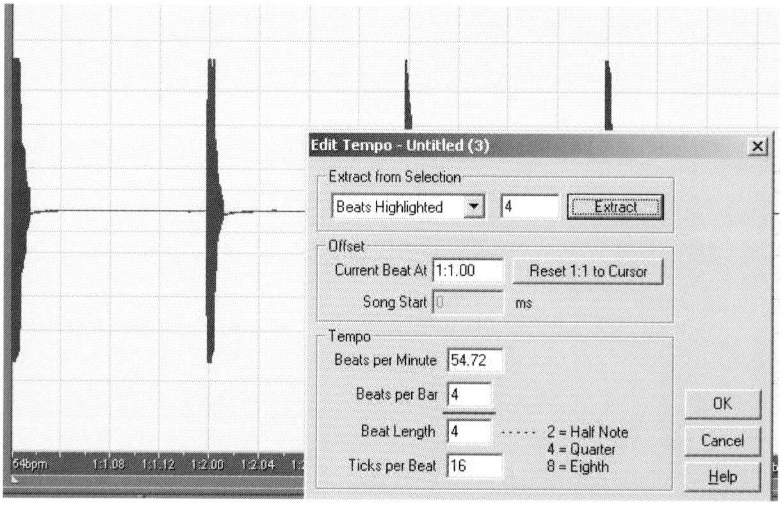

Figure 8.28
A simple one bar click is analysed to find the tempo.

In the Offset section you may reset the first beat of the first bar in the song to the current position of the cursor. Depending on the length of the waveblocks before the cursor this will produce a run in period before the start of the arrangement. (Assuming the arrangement starts at 00:00:00)

Usually the software makes a pretty good guess, depending on the source material of course. To view Bars and Beats in the Time Display Window right click on the ruler at the bottom of the waveform view and choose Display Time Format>Bars and Beats. The time display will now show bars, beats and ticks (clicks or count) as the playback cursor moves along the waveform. At this time the selected area does not have any looping information associated with it and so cannot be looped in the multitrack view. To enable looping:

1   Save the selection as a new file.
2   Close all files.
3   Open the loop file again and choose View Wave Properties.
4   In the Loop Info Box check that the values are correct and choose 'Loop'. Check that the value in 'Number of Beats' is OK.
5   In the Key section choose 'Non Voiced'.
6   In the Tempo Matching Section choose Beat Splice.
7   Press OK and resave the file ensuring that the option for saving extra non-audio information is checked.
8   Close the file again.
9   Switch to multitrack view and insert the file you have just saved.
10 Right click over the new waveblock and choose Loop Properties.
11 In the looping dialog set the loop interval to the number of beats in the waveform (usually 4 or 8). Check Follow session tempo and Lock position to Tempo are selected.
12 In the Multitrack View drag the extreme right of the waveblock along the session to create a looped section.

The looped waveform will adjust automatically to any changes in session tempo.

Analyze menu

The Analyze menu contains statistical tools for accurately measuring and displaying the frequency and amplitude content of a waveform.

Frequency analysis

A piece of music which is heavy in low frequency sound will be heard as being 'too bass heavy' or 'woolly' by the listener. A piece of music with too many high frequencies may be rejected as 'too tinny' or 'bright'. Balancing the frequencies in a piece of music is as much of an art form as balancing the amplitude. It's very difficult (almost impossible) to map frequency information over a piece of music and apply it successfully to another. However it is very useful to be able to see which frequencies are dominating a waveform in order to see problems that may not be apparent using the waveform view. The Frequency Analyser is a floating window (Figure 8.29) displaying a constantly updated view of the frequencies within a waveform.

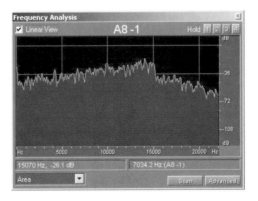

Figure 8.29
The Frequency Analyser is a floating window displaying a constantly updated view of the frequencies within a waveform.

To start the Frequency Analyser choose Analyse>Frequency from the menu bar. The frequency analyser tool is a small floating window with a descriptive graph. Frequency information appearing under the playback cursor is shown within the graph as a line. The line is curved to show the presence of more or less frequencies at each moment in time. The X axis shows the lowest frequencies to the left to the highest frequencies at the right. It's as if the spectral analysis window had tipped over onto it's back. The ruler at the bottom of the floating window no longer shows time but frequency content. With the Frequency Analysis window open, press play. The frequency curve will move as the playback cursor moves along the waveform on play. If the curve doesn't move check that a value of 2048 or 4096 exists within the FFT Size window and that Options>Show Levels on Play and Record is enabled.

Options for graph type, FFT size and analysis are shown underneath the graph. Use the Peak Hold buttons above the graph to mark the current shape of the graph. Four hold views are available. When playback is stopped the Frequency Analysis graph can be made to step through the waveform using the cursor keys left and right. Left and Right channel selections can be made using the keyboard up and down cursor keys.

Phase Analysis

Phase Analysis displays phase information in a similar way to the Frequency Analysis graph. The graph shows the difference in phase between the right and left channels of a stereo waveform. The x-axis (the bottom edge of the graph) represents the left channel's sample value, while the y-axis (the graph's right side) measures the sample value of the waveform's right channel.   The main use of this function is to make sure that the left and right channels won't have any phase cancellation. (H.Shafer)

Figure 8.30
The Phase Analysis graph shows the difference in phase between the right and left channels of a stereo waveform.

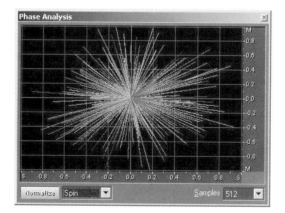

Statistics

Opens a non-floating window showing statistical details of the currently loaded waveform or selected range. Small 'arrows' on the General page point to the area in the data that have that value. For instance to see the sample in the wave that has the minimum value on the left side, click the adjacent arrow within the statistics dialog and the playback cursor will move to that point. The histogram page of this dialog features a graph indicating the high amplitudes within the data.

Even if you don't understand all of the information in the Statistics dialog it can still be used to create impressive results. For instance; creating professionally sounding CDs using home equipment is a tricky job. The impression of quality isn't just in the songs or the instruments but also in the balance between the songs themselves. The tracks on a commercially released album all peak at the same level and this makes it easier for the listener to simply enjoy the music without worrying about why some songs are quieter than others. It's also important if you want your CD's to sound great in the record company or radio station office.

Use the information within the statistics dialog to balance a series of waveforms without using the normalise function. If the entire compilation were normalised to the same values the overall level of the entire compilation would simply be raised to the maximum amplitude dictated by the highest peak in the entire compilation. So a chamber orchestra would be very quiet on the same CD as a surf punk track. This procedure normalises to RMS rather than to peak, enabling the entire compilation to sound even from one track to the next. Audio engineers who use this software always use this procedure when making CD compilations of songs.

RMS Normalising of CD compilation in preparation for burning

Firstly, create the CD compilation by pasting waveforms or using Open Append. Insert a two second gap at the front of each waveform if you plan to use the 'disk at once' method of burning. If the waveforms are not already converted to 32bit do this now or this procedure will not work. Save the entire waveform as a new file.

1 Open the Cue List (View>Cue List).
2 Double Click on the first range (range is selected in waveform view).
3 Choose Analyze>Statistics. Set the RMS Window width to 0ms and recalculate.
4 Note the average RMS power of the channel closest to 0dB (-8dB is louder than −10dB).
5 Close the statistics window and choose Transform>Amplitude>Amplify.
6 Ensure 'View All Settings in dB' and 'Lock Left/Right' are both checked.
7 Enter a value of minus the amount noted in the Waveform Satistics dialog box. Eg; if the louder of the two channels was −30dB a value of 30dB needs to be entered in the Amplify dialog. Click OK. (Note: The waveform will be overamplified. Don't panic!)
8 Repeat steps 2-7 for each of the cue ranges.
9 Edit>Select the entire wave.
10 Normalise the entire wave to 96%.
11 Batch process the Cue List to save each file individually.

Thanks to Drowz72 for permission to adapt his procedure for this book.

Tip

Many people save the finished files intended for burning to a 'publish' folder. This avoids expensive confusion when deciding which files to actually burn to the CD.

Options Menu

Loop Mode

Duplicates the action of press the 'loop' button on the transport bar.

Timed Record

Displays a non-floating window whereby Adobe Audition can be set to start recording at any time or date, for a set length of time depending on storage space available. To set these options enable Options>Timed Record and press the Record button on the toolbar. The red 'LED' set into the record button will flash when the program is 'armed' and waiting to start recording.

Monitor Record Level

Duplicates the action of pressing F10 on the computer keyboard. This option may also be found on the right click menu over the time display window. Additionally the option to Show Levels On Play and Record will enable the level meters automatically whenever Adobe Audition is in record or play mode.

MIDI Trigger Enable

Enables the software for the reception of MIDI messages which may be used to start or stop recording, etc. Alternatively, press Alt + 6 on the computer keyboard to enable MIDI input. Any feature within Adobe Audition can be controlled remotely using MIDI messages. For more information see the section entitled 'MIDI Triggering' later in this book.

Synchronise Cursor Across Windows

Use Synchronise Cursor when it's necessary to work at the same place in time along two or more waveforms. The playback cursor will appear at the same point in time in all loaded waveforms. Selected ranges will also appear in the same place in each loaded waveforms. If synchronise cursor is not enabled Adobe Audition will remember highlighted ranges within each open waveform.

Windows Recording Mixer

Invokes the standard Windows Recording Mixer control for the setting and checking of levels coming into the soundcard. Most soundcards are supplied with superior interfaces containing controls for features available only with that soundcard. However the Windows Mixer can be useful for simple level checking.

Start Default Windows CD Player

Invokes the standard Windows CD player. Use this feature if you have an older CD drive which cannot support digital 'ripping' of audio data from audio CD's. Because ripped data is purely digital and therefore loses nothing in the translation to it is preferable to use digitally ripped audio data over analogue information processed by the soundcard.

Scripts and Batch Processing

Adobe Audition is the only audio editor offering scripting and batch processing. These two features enable the advanced user to create custom macros to speed up the processing of repetitive tasks. For example. You have recorded one side of an LP for archiving. You have created cue ranges for each song on the LP and would like to apply click and pop elimination and normalizing to each song. A script that uses the currently selected range can be created to easily automate this task. Scripts can also be made to work with no waveform loaded (in which case the script must open a wave file), or to work on the whole currently loaded waveform. Nb. This procedure assumes that you have created a waveform containing the songs from one side of your LP and that you have created named cue ranges for each song.

Creating a script for a cue range or song

1 Open the Cue List window (View>Cue List) and double click on the first item in the Cue List, which should be your first song. The cue range is now highlighted.
2 Choose Options>Scripts and Batch Processing. Push the 'Open/New Collection' and choose a place to store your script and a name for the script collection. This can be a different name from the action of the script. For instance if you plan to make a few scripts to use when restoring vinyl you may choose 'Vinyl Toolkit' as a collection name.
3 Push the 'Open' button.
4 Type a descriptive name for this new de-clicker and normalize script in the Title dialog.
5 Push 'record'. From this point on the software will record your actions. Now edit the selected range as normal.
6 Choose Effects>Noise Reduction>Click and Pop Eliminator and apply the Old Record preset.
7 When finished, choose Effects>Amplitude>Normalize and normalize the selected range to 96%.
8 When the effects have been applied choose Options>Scripts>Batch Processing and push the 'Stop Current Script' button.
9 Type a short helpful description for the script including reminders of presets and values used if you like, then push the 'Add To Collection' button. The title of the script appears in the collections list.
10 Press 'Close'.

This script can now be used as a tool for each of the cue ranges in your waveform.

1 Return to the Cue List and double click the second song in the list.
2 Choose Options>Scripts and Batch Processing, Adobe Audition remembers the open collection and we can see our script title in the left hand window. Remember to remove the check mark from the option 'Pause At Dialogs' or you'll need to sit in front of the computer and press 'OK' to agree to every effect!
3 Click on the title of the script and press 'Run Script'.

The script runs and transforms our second song with no need for input. This is great as far as it goes but it's not completely automatic. Unfortunately we have to return to the computer after the script has run to select another range. What's needed is a way to edit all the songs, one at a time with no need for user input. Using the batch function in the Cue List, we can save each song as a different file. With the whole album saved in this way we can use scripts to work through each song, one at a time. For this we'll use the songs on the second side of the album and we'll assume that these have been recorded as before as one large waveform with cue ranges defined for each song.

Scripting for files using batch processing

1 Load the waveform for the second side.
2 Open the Cue List and shift click to select each of the cues.
3 With the cues selected press the merge button then the batch button.
4 In the Batch dialog (Figure 8.31) choose 'Save To Files'.
5 In the filename template type Song???. This tells Adobe Audition to call the saved files Song1, Song2, Song3, etc.
6 Choose a destination with enough space to store the saved files and choose Windows PCM as the output format.
7 Press OK and each cue range is saved as a new file.
8 Close all Open Waveforms and Sessions in Adobe Audition.

Figure 8.31
The Batch dialog.

Each of the cue ranges that were specified in the waveform has now been saved as a completely new waveform. A script can now be applied automatically to each of the files in turn.

1 Load the first song (Song1).
2 Return to Options>Scripts and Batch Processing and follow the procedure for creating a script from scratch as before. This script can be added to the current collection.
3 Work through each effect, open the Scripts dialog, stop the recording and add a description to this new script.
4 Push 'Add To Current Collection'.
5 Close the Scripts dialog and close but don't save the Song1 wave.
6 Close all open waveforms within Adobe Audition.
7 Choose Options>Scripts and Batch Processing.

8 Click on the title of the latest script and the text 'Script Works on Current Wave' appears at the bottom of the dialog to illustrate that this script is available for use on any open file. Because this is true the Batch Run button is enabled.

9 Push 'Batch Run' and push 'Add Files'.

10 Find your song files and using the normal windows shift+click or control+click technique, select the ones for processing.

11 Choose a destination with enough storage capacity for the new files and a suitable output format.

With everything in place press begin. Adobe Audition begins to process each file in turn, opening and saving as it works through, leaving the engineer time to do much more productive things. Like finding lunch!

Sharing and manually editing script files

As well as saving time now, scripts can be shared with other Adobe Audition users. Scripts are stored in easily understandable plain text files (*.scp). Script files can be copied, pasted or otherwise manipulated just like any other text document and stored anywhere on the computer or LAN. Store in data disk or partition for safety. To manually edit a script from within the Scripts and Batch Processing dialog box push the 'Edit Script File' button. This causes Windows Notepad to open with the contents of the current script file. Otherwise simply open script file with Notepad.

Renaming a script

Every collection is simply called 'New Collection' when created. Rename the collection by editing the text after the colon: in the first line of the script file. The new title is now seen whenever the script file is loaded.

```
Title: Title belongs here
Description: Describe purpose of script in as many lines as you wish
Description: These lines are displayed in script dialog
cmd:
1:
2:
3:
4:
5:
6:
End:
```

Tip

If your system partition or disk suffers a failure you can always reinstall the software. But any scripts you make will be lost. If you can, always choose another partition or disk to for your personal data.

Adobe Audition is supplied with three example scripts in C:\Program Files\Adobe\Audition 1.0\Scripts

Favourites

It takes only a short while to get used to working with Adobe Audition. Most users have a favourite set of commands and procedures that they use on almost every file and find that they can save time by creating shortcuts to their favourite procedures using the Edit Favourites feature.

To create a shortcut that will normalise a file to −3db using just two keystrokes.

1 In the Edit Menu choose Favourites>Edit Favourites from the main menu bar.
2 Press New and enter Normalise to −3dB in the Name property box.
3 Click once in the shortcut property box, press and hold the Alt key on the keyboard and tap the N key once. Alt+N will appear in the shortcut box as your keystroke to invoke this shortcut.
4 Choose the Function tab and navigate the drop down list until you find Amplitude/Normalize.
5 Press the Edit Settings box and set the normalize parameters to −3dB equally. Press OK to return to the Favorites dialog.
6 Make sure that the Show Dialog box is not checked.
7 Press Save to save this as a favourite.

Now whenever you are in the Edit View you may normalise any file to −3dB simply by pressing Alt+N. Favourites may also be made to invoke other programs. For instance to invoke the Windows Notepad with a shortcut choose the Tool tab in the Favorites dialog and enter c:\windows\notepad.exe in the command line. Using the Favourites feature it is easy to build and create a menu of your favourite and most useful commands, tools and third party programs.

Real time effects and mixers

Real time effects enable the user to overlay effects on top of waveforms in the multitrack view. Mixers simulate the traditional way that an audio engineer would use a large console with a long fader for each channel. This isn't necessary in the PC environment but many users feel more comfortable when using software with a mixer view.

Differences between effects in Edit View and Multitrack View

Edit View

In Edit View the effects are applied one after another. Every effect that is applied alters the sound of the effect applied before it. For instance a reverb effect applied after an echo would add a reverb tail to each repeat. An echo applied after a reverb would have many repeats each containing a little reverb. The most natural sounding effect would be to apply reverb after the echo. Effects applied in Edit View are destructive; that is that the effect is saved into the waveform. If you decide the effect doesn't suit for some reason after the session has been saved, that's it. The waveform will have been changed forever and there's no going back. The lesson of course is make a backup! The upside to this is that effects applied in Edit View can sound better than those in Multitrack View as the PC only has to handle one at a time. So make your waveform sound killer in Edit View and let your computer relax.

- Effects are cumulative
- Effects are destructive
- Effects cannot be changed when in multitrack view
- Effects often sound more natural

Multitrack View

Effects in multitrack view are applied in real time and are non-destructive. In other words the effects are applied 'over' the waveblock as if the waveblock were put through additional software or hardware. However because the effects are included in the software some of the effects can interact with waveblocks in the session. These are called 'dynamic effects'. Dynamic effects can be made to change the sound of a waveform gradually over time for instance applying EQ filters to a drum track to create a wah-wah effect. Effects in the multitrack view are non destructive; they can be removed at any time even after the session has been saved. However, the additional load imposed on the processor can slow down or even stop background mixing and can cause slower systems to crash. This isn't a design fault – it happens to every single computer audio system and is sometimes caused by the users expectations (or the artists demands) exceeding the capabilities of the host system. Get used to what your system can do and if necessary buy more RAM or processing power to handle the artists' demands for five different true stereo reverbs over their vocal. Finally, effects applied in the multitrack view may sound a little less smooth than effects applied in the Edit View.

- Effects are applied in real time, after the waveform has been saved and do not affect the source waveform
- Effects can be chained in series or parallel
- Effects are not destructive
- Effects can slow down the computer
- Effects may not sound so good

Effects are applied in three ways in the multitrack view:

1 Modulation effects
2 Effects Racks
3 Effects applied over a buss

Modulation effects

Modulation effects process a waveblock using frequency or amplitude information from another waveblock. Three modulation effects are available in the multitrack view.

Envelope Follower

Used to create 'side chain' effects normally created in hardware using a noisegate triggered by 'key input' from a side chain source. For example, to create the chopped guitar effect typical of UK dance records from the late eighties.

1 Create a drum loop on track one.
2 Add a 'staggered' percussion part using a sound with plenty of attack such as a drumstick or cowbell. Record this on track two.
3 On track three record a sustained guitar part. Power chords are best, held for four or eight beats.
4 Save the session and waveforms and give each waveform a meaningful name such as drums, click, etc.
5 Use the mouse to draw a box over the waveblocks in tracks two and three from the top left of track two to the bottom right of track three. This will select a range over both tracks.
6 Choose Effects>Envelope Follower from the menu bar (Figure 9.1).
7 In the dialog select 'click' as the analysis wave and 'guitar' as the process wave. Output to any empty track and draw a gentle compression curve in the graph before pressing OK.

The chopped guitar effect will appear on the empty track.

Tip

If the session becomes heavy with resources and background mixing starts to slow down right click over the mix gauge and raise the priority of the background mix. If you make many tiny envelope changes and don't want to wait for background mixing to catch up each time disable background mixing until you want to play your session.

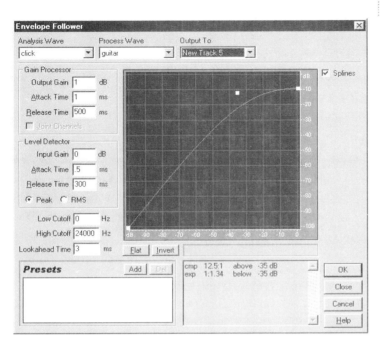

Figure 9.1
Envelope Follower is used to create 'side chain' effects normally created in hardware.

The envelope follower takes a few attempts before the results come right but it's a cheap and useful way to create these effects. Use the graph in the dialog box to draw curves similar to the Dynamics Processing effect and experiment with the high and low cutoff to create glassy chopping sounds. If your analysis wave is a loop (or duplicated waveblocks) you'll find that the results are only as long as the original source waveform. Either mixdown the looped sounds to one long waveform or use some other track length analysis wave.

Vocoder

The Vocoder creates retro sounding effects as a voice or sung part takes on the frequency content of another wave. Like the envelope follower it's best when used with rhythmic parts.

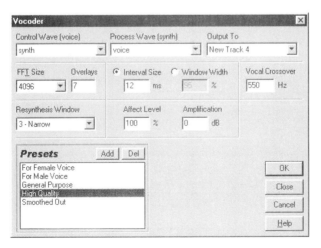

Figure 9.2
The Vocoder creates retro sounding effects as a voice or sung part takes on the frequency content of another wave.

1 Record a long sustained pad on track one using. Big analogue sounds with plenty of filter work well.
2 Record any vocal line on track two.
3 Draw a box from the top left of the waveblock in track one to the bottom right of the waveblock in track two. This action selects both waveblocks and creates a range within which the effect will be applied.
4 Within the Vocoder dialog either choose a preset or enter your own parameters for the process.

Frequency Band Splitter

The Frequency Band Splitter (Figure 9.3) is applied to single waveblocks only. Use this effect to produce new waveforms containing only certain frequencies of the process waveblock. This may be useful if you want to create complex delay effects using only some frequencies contained in the source.

Manually offset waveblocks to create delay effects

1 Record an arpeggio or rhythmic part into track one.
2 Drag select over the new waveblock and choose Effects>Frequency Band Splitter from the main menu.
3 Check four or five radio buttons in the right hand side of the dialog box. Each radio button generates a different waveblock containing only those frequencies.
4 Click OK and return to the multitrack view. New waveblocks have appeared in tracks two to four.
5 Click once on the waveblock in track two and right click. Choose Waveblock Properties from the right click menu.
6 In time offset add a hundred milliseconds to the figure shown. The display is in the same format as the display time window so if the offset isn't showing in decimal return to the multitrack display and right click over the display time window to choose the decimal format.
7 Click once on the waveblock in track three and add two hundred milliseconds to the time offset.
8 Do the same to tracks three and four adding a hundred milliseconds more each time.

Figure 9.3
The Frequency Band Splitter is used to produce new waveforms containing only certain frequencies of the process waveblock.

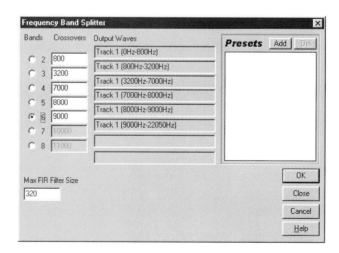

Mute the original waveform in track one and play the session to hear the delayed and split effect. For even more drama pan each waveblock and add echo to the high frequencies.

Direct X Effects, plug-ins and effects from other software

Direct X and other non-native effects can easily be applied in the multitrack view through the effects racks. Adobe Audition is able to use Direct X effects directly. After installing a new Direct X effect it is necessary to refresh the effects list to add the new effect. In the Edit View choose Effects>Refresh from the menu bar. It is even possible to use VST effects through the use of 'wrapper' software such as Spin Audio VST-DX Wrapper Lite (http://www.spinaudio.com).

Track Mixer

In the Multitrack View choose View>Mixers Window to see the mixer (Figure 9.4). The Mixers window shows track controls and properties for each track laid out in table form. This is intended to make mixing the session easier than having to switch between different track controls during your session. The Mixers window also features a 'Bus Mixer' tab containing track properties for each buss you may have created in that session.

Figure 9.4
The Mixers window shows track controls and properties for each track laid out in table form.

Within the track mixer are five view selection buttons. Each of these reveals or hides properties for every track; FX, EQ, Pan, etc. Using these buttons and by resizing the window it is possible to adjust the size of the Mixers window to suit your environment. The Mixers window also contains the master fader for the Adobe Audition session that used to be situated at the top of the Multitrack View.

Using the Mixers window to control and mix the session

Faders in the Mixers window may be controlled in the following ways:

- Using the arrows above and below the fader
- Dragging the fader manually
- Right clicking on the calibration produces a smooth fade
- Left clicking on the calibration produces a jump in level
- Overtyping values directly
- Right clicking on the fader 'button' produces a 'zero' option

Panning in the Mixers window may be controlled in the following ways:

- Dragging over the values in the Pan properties
- Using the 'toggle' just above the pan value to jump from left to right or to centre

Control EQ in the mixers window by dragging over the values in the H (high), M (Mid) and L (Low) properties.

Access properties for track effects using the FX buttons in the Mixers window.

Wet and Dry values for track effects are controlled in the individual track controls in Multitrack View. The FX values here control Buss effects only.

Each fader in the Mixers window has a small arrow immediately above and below the fader. Click once on the arrow to adjust

Busses

Busses enable track outputs to be routed together and through additional effects before reaching the sound card. In this way it's possible to group together track outputs and put them under the control of just one fader. This is useful when dealing with associated parts that may be grouped, such as a string section for instance.

Figure 9.5
A new bus has been created from the Mixer window.

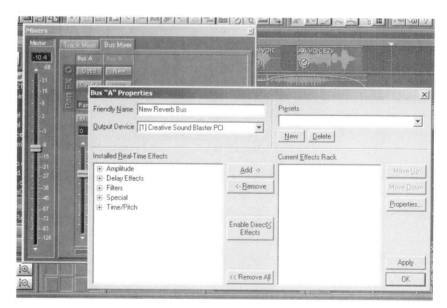

Busses must be created before they can be used and are created by left clicking over the Out button within the track controls for each track. The playback devices dialog will appear with any created busses in this session listed at the bottom of the dialog. Push the New Buss button to create a brand new bus.

The Bus Properties dialog (Figure 9.5) shows buss options. Essentially these are the same as the effect rack options with the addition of an output device select. This lists physical output devices inside the computer. Note that it is not necessary to have a sound card with multiple outputs to take advantage of the Buss system. To see properties and controls for the effects within the buss click on any of the loaded effects in the chain and click the properties button.

Give the new buss a friendly name and combine effects for the buss if you wish. The output device is now shown as 'Bus A' and the track will output through that buss. Note that effects are generated for the track first before being passed to the buss. The 'Bus' view select button in track controls now shows 'wet' and 'dry' values for that bus indicating that effects are enabled in the buss. Although any number of tracks may be routed through a single buss different wet and dry values for the effects in that bus may be set in the track controls dialog. This is similar to the 'effects send' control on a regular mixer. The effects rack mixer in the effects properties for the buss sets an effect 'return' for the buss.

Busses can be saved within sessions but cannot be copied from one session to another.

Bus Mixer

Access routing properties for the buss through the buttons at the top of the Bus Mixer. Effects properties and controls for each bus are viewed by pressing the Config button.

Like the mixer, each fader has a small arrow immediately above and below the fader. Click once on the arrow to adjust

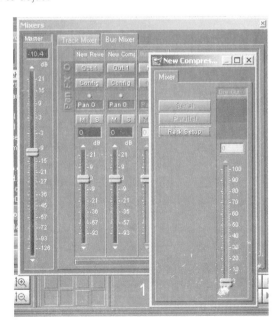

Figure 9.6
Two new busses have been created for applying effects to more than one track.

Automation

Adobe Audition includes automation for volume, pan and other effects through the use of envelopes in the multitrack view. The envelopes can be seen in each waveblock but these changes are not shown in the track properties, as envelope editing is a waveblock property. The track faders should also be seen as master faders for the track. The easiest way to understand this philosophy is to view envelope editing, including effects parameters, crossfading and panning just as part of the performance, as if they were recorded into the original waveform contained and controlled by waveblocks in each individual track. Just as individual performance dynamics can't be automated in a regular mixing environment, so envelope editing isn't seen or automated in the Track Mixer.

Track Mixer response

During playback of a multitrack session Adobe Audition is rendering constantly in the background. Button actions such as Mute, Solo etc. don't have an immediate effect because of this process. Typically a delay of about 500ms occurs between the button action and the effect. By tuning your installation of Adobe Audition to suit your system and the session it is possible to make Adobe Audition much more responsive to your mouse clicks and actions.

Bring up the Settings dialog using Options>Settings from the menu bar or by pressing F4 on the keyboard.

1   Set Playback Buffer (Response time) to a smaller value. Try a value between 1 second and 0.2 seconds.
2   Increase playback buffers to 20.
3   Decrease the background mixing priority level to 4.

At time of writing I am using a bespoke system based on an Athlon 1.4GHz processor with 1GB RAM and a 60MB A/V hard disk. The above settings increased the response time of Adobe Audition dramatically to the point where I was almost able to consider using the Track Mixers window as a tool to be used while mastering to DAT rather than simply an alternative means to set track properties. Although the performance of Adobe Audition was enhanced by these settings I did notice additional artifacts being introduced during extreme manipulation of the controls. My test session has 12 tracks of which three are muted and two have effects racks enabled.

Info

Settings are peculiar to your session and the resources available to the host computer.

Mixdown and mastering your soundtrack

Congratulations! By now you'll have become an expert in Adobe Audition and you'll have discovered for yourself just how powerful this software can be. Some new users are bemused by this unique approach to audio. Instead of handing the user a few simple tools complete with images of wood grain and screw holes, Adobe Audition enables the audio engineer to create the real tools he or she needs to get the job done. You've discovered how to make your own effects, more special than almost anything you can buy and you've also discovered how to produce and manipulate hundreds of waveforms at the same time – without the need for a multiple output sound card. By now you'll hopefully have some audio that you'd like other people to hear. Sometimes audio produced by inexperienced engineers can sound a little hard on the ears. Maybe too much bass or treble, or not loud enough when played back through a domestic stereo system. All these production problems have a solution and Adobe Audition provides the tools to make it work.

Creating a finished product

Mastering is an audio term for producing a mix that is balanced in EQ and amplitude along the length of the soundtrack or song. Mastering is where you create your finished product ready for distribution so it must be tailored for that distribution. This might mean inserting track indexes for a CD master or using Hard Limiting to ensure that the piece of music is ear catching enough to complete on the FM airwaves. There may easily be several mastered versions of the same project.

Creating a finished product involves the following steps:

- Recording the waveforms
- Editing the waveforms
- Editing the waveblocks referencing the waveforms and arranging them into a session
- Balancing volume, pan, EQ and adding effects if necessary
- Creating a final single stereo waveform containing all the ingredients of the session. This is called 'mixing down'

Mixing down is the process whereby one session length waveform is created from the contents of all waveblocks in a session including the values in track controls such as effects, volume and pan. Buss parameters and effects are also mixed into the new waveform. The final stereo wav is suitable for burning to CD, making available on a website, encoding as MP3 or any other means of electronic distribution.

Saving a mixdown

Adobe Audition provides the following routes for rendering two or more waveblocks together into one mixdown wave.

File>Save Mixdown As

Creates a new wav file containing contents of all waveblocks, effects, etc. Prompts for a filename before saving mixdown.

Edit>Mixdown>All Waves

Has the same effect as the first option and also loads mixdown wav into Edit View without saving.

Edit>Mixdown>Selected Waves

As above but only mixes content of selected waves.

Edit>Mixdown>All Waves Mono

Creates and loads a mono waveform

Edit>Mixdown>Selected Waves Mono

As above but only of selected waves.

Bouncing to free resources

Files can also be 'bounced' to create a complete mixdown of the session including effects and envelopes etc. in the first available free track. In this way tracks with many effects or envelopes can be preserved to free resources.

If no range is selected Edit>Mixdown will create a waveform from the very beginning of the session to the end of the last waveblock. If a range has been selected a waveform is created of the contents of the range. Using selected waves and a range it is possible to create alternative loops and phrases of just part of your session for use in later projects.

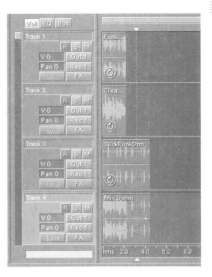

Figure 10.1
Three .cel loops have been bounced down. A mixdown file has automatically been created in track four.

Real time mixing

The mixdown is rendered immediately and track mixers, etc. are disabled at this time. Therefore to include crossfades and fadeouts, etc. it is necessary to program these in using envelopes before the mixdown is created. At the end of this process you will have a single stereo waveform of your entire mix ready for post production.

Post production

Post Production is where your session mix waveform turns into something that everyone can hear. Normally, a mixdown waveform needs a little smoothing before being released from the controlled environment of the recording studio. The dynamic range will need to be adjusted, the beginning and ends will need to be tailored to fit and sometimes a little EQ may need to be added or taken away (not too much, EQ is a production decision which needs to have been made before the session was saved in stone at mixdown!)

EQ and effects

Post Production EQ is only ever applied in tiny amounts and usually to correct a specific problem that wasn't noticed during the recording. One common problem with most semi-professional mixes is that two or more instruments may be fighting for the same space in the frequency range. Sometimes this may work – guitar and snare drum or bass and kick drum are two classic examples of instruments complimenting each other. However brass section, guitar and vocals almost always need to sit alongside each other yet all occupy that harsh middle ground. The solution to this is to prioritise. Return to the session and identify the parts that are banging into each other. Decide which is the most crucial to the song or that part of the song and either mute the other parts for that section or use another device such as panning instruments in the same frequency range or frequency splitting to create space inside the mix. Use panning to create excitement and motion for the part while adding space to the crowded frequency range at the same time. Use the Pan Expand effect from the Amplitude selection for complex expanding effects.

Info

Some freely available third party mastering tools become very useful at this stage of the recording. Check Dave Brown's Audioware website for his very useful Mastering Limiter, Tempo Delay and other high quality tools for the broadcast industry; http://www.db-audioware.com

Alternatively simply enable Envelope Editing and draw panning envelopes directly onto the waveform.

Expert users recommend enhancing the mixdown waveform through the use of EQ before using the dynamics processor. Key frequencies are:

60Hz–80Hz	(bass, 45hz and below for sub-bottom)
250Hz	(muddiness/low mid)
1.25k–2.5k	(vocal fundamental)
5.8k/6.3k	(sibilance)
8k–14k	(presence and shimmer)

Use less than 3db of cut or boost in any frequency band.

First steps

1 Normalise to −3db if necessary. Normalising is necessary if the resulting mixdown file peaks below −20db. A production destined for the Top 40 should already be finely balanced to ensure that no part of the waveform exceeds −0 dB and that lower amplitude sections aren't confusing to hear.
2 Convert your mixdown file to 32bit if not done already.
3 Trim leading space and trailing space. Be careful when removing trailing space as very low amplitude noise is difficult to see at long distance.

Adding 'air' to a vocal line

It's possible to bring 'air' into a vocal if you use the parametric equaliser (Figure 10.2) to remove just .5db of 12500kHz (1.25k). In the Edit View use Effects>Silence to remove clicks and coughs etc, between lines.

1 Double click the waveblock in Multitrack View to load the waveform into Edit View.
2 Select the area to be silenced.
3 Choose Effects>Silence from the menu bar.

While it is easy to remove all additional noise in this way many producers prefer to leave breath sounds etc. believing they add to the natural feel of the vocal line.

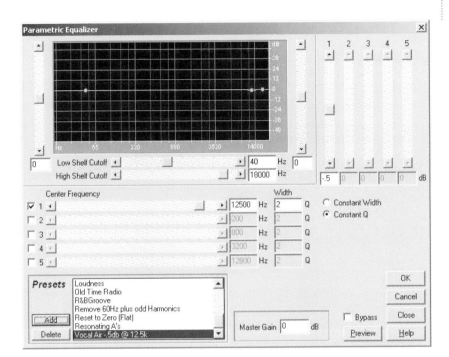

Figure 10.2
Use the parametric equaliser to bring 'air' into a vocal line.

Additional vocal techniques

Use volume envelopes to bring life to a vocal line. This technique is a 'low tech' attempt to do manually what compressors were invented to do automatically. However because no compressor has the processing power of the human brain (yet) we are able to manipulate the envelopes to enhance the feel as well as the dynamics of the performance.

1 Select the vocal phrase or line for editing and zoom to selection. Zoom in vertically to create lots of room for editing.
2 Enable Envelope Editing and Show Volume Envelopes
3 Drag the volume envelope two thirds of the way down the waveform. This is necessary as the volume envelope only attenuates the waveblock – it doesn't add gain. To create a lift in volume it's necessary to reduce the overall level first to allow some headroom.
4 Right Click over the waveblock and choose Use Spline Envelope for Volume.
5 Using the waveform display as a guide, create volume envelopes over each phrase lifting the ends of words and dipping where necessary to remove attack. Click on the line to add handles, drag handles off the waveblock to remove.
6 Compensate for the volume envelope by adding 2 or 3dB of gain in Track Properties.
7 To remove all handles right click over the waveblock and select Clear Envelope.

The effect is subtle but it will enhance any vocal line and make you (the engineer/producer) into a hero in the eyes of the singer!

Lo fi vocals

No computer is ever going to replace a vintage analogue compressor, but a few tweaks will send an ordinary vocal into lo-fi madness.

1   Heavily compress the plain vocal using these parameters:

Cmp 7.03 : 1   above −22.5 dB
Cmp 2.92 : 1   below −22.5 dB

2   Distort the compressed vocal using Effects>Special>Distortion. I found the Bow Curve 2 preset to be good for producing the lo-fi effect.

3   Any number of files can be opened at the same time in Edit View but only one file at a time may be edited. Save the treated vocal (but don't close) and use File>New to create a brand new 44.1/32bit mono file.

4   In the new file use Generate>Noise to create background noise with the following parameters:

Colour   Brown
Intensity   3.3
Duration   As long as the vocal wave to be treated

5   Edit>Copy the contents of this wave and return to the vocal by choosing the file name from the Window menu on the menu bar. This will return to the already open vocal wave without closing the newly created noise wave.

6   Edit>Mix Paste the contents of the clipboard into the vocal wave. Choose 100% volume and Overlap as the mix type. If your noise wave isn't long enough you can choose to repeat (loop) the pasted wave as many times as necessary to cover the entire vocal.

Alternatively copy a sample of a scratched record and mix paste this into the vocal for an authentically 'old' sound. For enhanced 'grunge' authenticity create a waveform containing some 60 cycle hum (Generate>Tones) and mix paste this at a low level into the vocal waveform also.

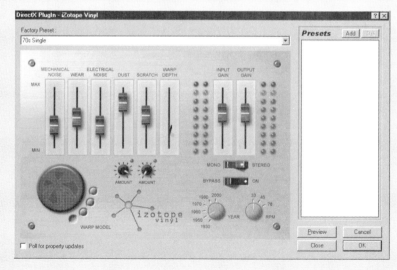

The iZotope Vinyl Direct X plugin is almost unbeatable for creating lo-fi masterpieces from your beautifully recorded 24/96 works of art! Available free from http://www.izotope.com

Fixing the bass

Bass and getting the right amount of the right sort of bass has to be the number one question. Only experience will tell you when you have the mix just right but there are a few things you can do to make sure things are going in the right direction.

- Listen to mixes on a variety of systems. Car hi-fi, living room hi-fi, boom box etc. Many people have a set of cheaper speakers or even a portable stereo in the control room just for this.
- Take a break from time to time and compare your mix against a contemporary Top 40 CD or something that you are familiar with. The reality check is always useful.
- Periodically monitor at very low levels.
- Carefully compress low end (bass) drums using Dynamics Processing to retain the high end while ensuring the low end is not overpowering.
- Create several mixes with slightly differing amounts of kick drum to bass guitar ratio. Make sure the kick drum and bass guitar sit tightly together. Use the Envelope Follower in Multitrack session to create a sidechain effect.

The golden rule is not to boost any frequency below 100hz by more than 3dB unless the waveform absolutely demands it. Boosting bass frequencies artificially, even in an environment such as Adobe Audition is no different to hitting the 'Mega Bass' button on a cheap hi-fi. The result will be that you mix will sound bass heavy through your speakers but take that mix anywhere else, to a club or even a friend's stereo system and the boosted bass frequencies will obscure everything.

Adjusting dynamic range using Dynamics Processing

Dynamic range is the difference between the loudest and the quietest or softest sounds in a piece. For example classical music has a very wide dynamic range while contemporary pop music almost always has a very small dynamic range. This is because pop music is made to grab and hopefully hold our attention for just long enough for us to want to buy the product. Music with a small dynamic range translates easily to smaller inexpensive systems such as in a car or a radio. Music with a wide dynamic range requires a more expensive system to sound truthful. Most productions benefit from some degree of dynamic range adjustment.

1 Select the entire waveform or ensure that the Default Selection Range is set to Entire Wave in Adobe Audition Settings (F4).
2 Choose Effects>Amplitude>Dynamics Processing.

Use the Dynamics Processing transform to apply just enough compression to bring the lowest or quietest parts of the waveform up to a point where they would remain audible even if the finished mix were to be played at low volume. Use the splines feature to create easy compression curves. Avoid the temptation to add too much makeup gain at this stage. The highest parts of the waveform should remain at below −3dB to avoid clipping. Use the create envelope only feature to hear the effect of the compression curve on the waveform. A gentle compression will cause the white noise to 'ripple' in time with the music. Create two 'nodes' with the following values:

	Node1	Node2
Input Signal Level	−15.6	0
Output Signal Level	−8.7	-6.8

In the Attack/Release tab enter the following values:

Output Gain	−2
Attack Time	26ms
Release Time	100ms

Edit values until the difference between low and high amplitude portions of the wave is slightly reduced. Applying too much compression will make the sound flat and lifeless. This can be seen as well as heard (picture of over compressed waveform and slightly compressed waveform).

It's a controversial thing to discuss but in general most people like their mixes to appear very 'loud'. Certainly, if your production is destined for a Top 40 radio station or a record company executive the mix must be as punchy and attention grabbing as possible. The Hard Limiter effect will raise the maximum amplitude of a file to -.5db or as near to clipping as it's possible to get. Use the Hard Limiter to squash the dynamic range right down to bring the entire mix right into the foreground. Remember to record several versions and call the hard limited version the 'Radio Mix' and don't use it on the album!

Production techniques

Dynamic Processing is invaluable for smoothing out an irregular waveform or for making the track seem more powerful but it can't replace the care and imagination that can bring life to a lifeless track when balancing the session in Multitrack View. Because it's not possible to 'ride' the faders like a hardware mixer, take extra time with volume envelopes and splitting and muting portions of a waveblock in the session. Muting a key instrument and dramatically reintroducing it later can add excitement to a song.

- In the Multitrack View, place the mouse cursor over the yellow handle at the top of the playback cursor and drag to wherever the split should happen. Or simply click at the appropriate point.
- Right click and choose 'Split' from the menu. The entire waveblock on both sides of the split will now be selected.
- Click on any empty space in the session to deselect the waveblock.
- Right click over the portion of the waveblock to be muted and select 'Mute Block'.

Split sections can be grouped together and moved as a group.

Normalise

Normalise the mixdown waveform in preparation for the final stage of post production. Adobe Audition files are accurate and intended for use with high quality hardware and CD burning software. Experiment with normalising to 100% but listen to the results closely. Most software and burning hardware will handle files normalised to %98 without problems.

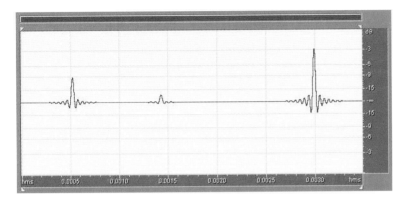

Figure 10.3
This waveform has three peaks. The rightmost peak is almost at maximum amplititude.

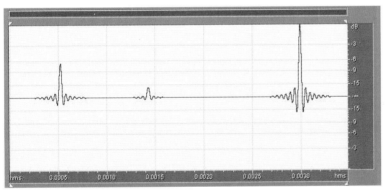

Figure 10.4
After normalising to 99.5% the waveform has been normalised to the amplitude of the highest peak.

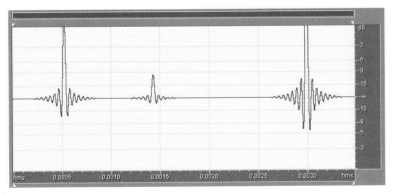

Figure 10.5
Dynamics processing has raised the amplitude of the lower peak to almost the same value as the highest.

Creating a waveform in preparation for burning to CD

Waveforms with 32bit (44.1/32) resolution will need to be converted to a format compatible with CD Burning software and other means of electronic distribution. Only audio saved in 44.1 kHz 16bit (44.1/16) format is suitable for CD burning. As we have been working in 32 bits up until now it's necessary to convert the sample type to 16 Bits before continuing. Choose Edit>Convert Sample Type from the menu bar. Choose the following options.

- 44100 kHz
- Stereo
- 16 Bit
- Enable Dithering
- Dither Depth 0.7 bits (Syntrillium recommend values between 0.2 and 0.7. Experiment for best results)
- Pdf is Triangular
- Noise Shaping curve preset is 44.1KHz

Save the waveform and use with any quality CD burning program to create your soundtrack CD. Some CD software comes with recommendations for your audio. These shouldn't be used if you have prepared your waveform with Adobe Audition.

MP3 file encoding

MP3 file format enables audio to be compressed into very easily managed file sizes suitable for MP3 players, iPod, Car MP3 players etc. Make sure that you encode your audio with title, genre and copyright information using the Edit>Waveform Properties tools in the Edit View. Files need to be converted down from 32 bit to 16 bit before encoding. To encode as an MP3 file use File>Save As and choose MPEG 3 (FhG) from the Save As Type drop down box. Push the 'Options' button to see options for the encoded file. Choose CBR encoding (Constant Bit Rate) unless the file will only ever be duplicated and transmitted within a controlled environment (a company wide WAN for instance). Options for file sizes are chosen from the drop down box and should be set according to your means of distribution, bandwidth capabilities etc. Most common is 128 kbps 44100Hz Stereo. Stereo files can be converted to mono during this process.

That's it and good luck!

That's it for this book. Together we've gone through creating your soundtrack, editing and adding effects right into recording and mastering and creating sounds of your own. Adobe Audition is much more than a simple waveform editing and rendering tool. It offers you the ability to powerfully sculpt your own aural environment and to create industry standard mixes of that environment that stand up to the closest scrutiny.

I hope you enjoy making music with your new software and I wish you success with your projects.

Advanced configuration

Advanced configuration

Most times Adobe Audition will run fine right out of the box. In fact this software has a reputation for running on systems that can't handle any other audio editor. However if you have an older PC you may find a smoother ride if you adjust some system settings within Adobe Audition itself. The best time to do this is right now after installation. This part of the book contains help on tailoring your copy of Adobe Audition to suit your PC and system. Incidentally, Adobe Audition won't adjust itself automatically so if you add additional RAM, etc. you'll need to revisit this section. Also, remember to use the excellent help system. It offers detailed descriptions of each option within this dialog. Press F1 on your keyboard to see context sensitive help wherever you are in the program.

These options are found in the system options dialog box under Options>Settings from the toolbar or by pushing F4 on the computer keyboard. It is older systems running older versions of Windows (95 or 98) that will benefit mostly from these settings.

1 General settings

Show Tip Of The Day

Choose to see the Adobe 'Tip Of The Day' whenever Audition starts. Most users choose not to see these after a short while but new users may find these tips useful. Optional

Use Shiny Look

Completely optional setting for producing a metallic look to buttons etc. Has no performance hit whatsoever. Optional.

Auto Play On Command Line Load

May be used to force Audition to play any file in any valid format when the program starts. Choose Start Button>Run and enter the following in the Run dialog box 'C:\Program Files\Adobe\Audition 1.0\audition.exe' myfile.wav Please note that the quotation marks before and after the file path are necessary. Please substitute any valid file name for 'myfile.wav' but ensure that the file is in the Audition folder.

Figure 11.1
General settings

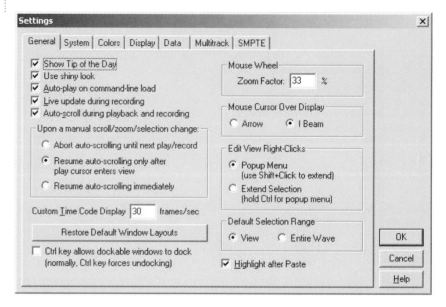

Live Update During Record

Enables Audition to display the waveform as it is recorded. Essential for troubleshooting during the recording process but can be turned off if system resources are low.

Auto Scroll During Play and Record

Enables Audition to scroll the waveform in time with playback. Optional. Please note scrolling will only occur if a small portion of the waveblock is viewed and if 'Play To End' not 'Play' is chosen.

Upon A Manual/Zoom/Selection Change

Affects auto scroll behaviour after one of the three conditions are met. In other words should you zoom into a waveform you may choose here what happens to the Auto Scroll feature on the next instance of play.

Custom Time Code Display

Adobe Audition will use a custom frames per second (FPS) frame rate if one is set here. This value is assigned to the Custom time format.

Restore Default Window Layouts

Adobe Audition features dockable windows that may be dragged around the screen to alternative locations. This feature is useful at times when you may wish to monitor or view windows that are minimised or hidden but can become confused if you have many windows floating around the screen. Use this option to restore the default layout.

Ctrl Key allows dockable windows to dock

Normally, holding down the Ctrl key on the keyboard will prevent windows from automatically docking (joining together) if they pass.

Mouse Wheel zoom factor

If you have an Intellipoint mouse you may choose how far to zoom in when rotating the mouse wheel. Higher numbers indicate a closer zoom.

Mouse Cursor Over Display

Enables Audition to produce an I Beam or just an arrow when held over the waveform display. Many users find that the I Beam enables greater control over cut points and selections.

Edit View Right Clicks

Enables one of two options when rightclicking over a waveform in the Edit View. The Popup menu shows a menu of options while the Extend Selection option enables the selection to be extended to the right. IF this option is chosen you may also use Ctrl+Right Click to view the popup menu. This is a personal preference but I choose the Extend Selection option.

Default Selection Range

Adobe Audition can catch you out particularly if you have selected just a portion of a waveform for editing. It's possible to spend some time getting that waveform to sound just great and even to save it without realising that the portions of the waveform that are not visible have also NOT been affected by your edits and effects. Choose the 'Entire Wave' option to ensure that everything you are doing is affecting the whole waveform but beware – sometimes you may NOT wish to add a huge reverb over your entire 40 minute drum solo in which case check to ensure that you have 'View' only selected.

Highlight After Paste

After pasting a selection of a waveform over another you can choose whether to have Adobe Audition highlight (select) the newly pasted portion of the wave or simply to set the cursor at the right of the pasted area. Generally it is more useful to see where your new section is so leave this option checked.

2 System settings

The system settings affect the performance of Adobe Audition. Make a note of the default settings so you have a 'known good' configuration if the PC becomes uncontrollable.

Play Record Buffer

Buffers are areas of physical memory reserved or used by the program to store audio ready for playback or recording after it has been rendered. In a powerful computer with a good quality soundcard the default values may be used with little problem. However in an older PC you may wish to adjust these properties to smooth the performance of Adobe Audition. If you experience 'choppiness' or stuttering and dropouts in playback you may find that increasing the number of buffers (in seconds) and buffer size may help. Increasing buffer sizes will take more of the physical memory required by other processes so the amount available is not unlimited. A setting of 10, 1 second buffers is a good place to start.

Figure 11.2
System settings

Wave Cache

This value is the amount of memory reserved by Adobe Audition for the data buffer. The size of the buffer is dependent on the amount of physical memory inside your computer. Larger buffers are better. Use the following table to determine the cache size suitable for your PC. You should seriously consider upgrading if your PC has less than 64MB of RAM. For PC's like this use the lowest value of 8192.

64MB RAM	8192
96MB RAM	12288
128MB RAM	16384
256MB RAM	32768

Use System Cache

Use this option only if your PC has less than 64MB of physical memory. This option will enable Windows to handle all disk caching and so (hopefully) allocate just enough memory for all the processes.

Preview Buffer

Most of the Adobe Audition effects have a preview feature. This value is the minimum size of the preview buffer. The default is 1000ms but this can be reduced if you experience dropouts or stutter when previewing effects.

Temporary Folders

Adobe Audition creates large temporary files for undo and recovery information. The location of these files is set in these fields. Choose the largest and fastest physical disk available. Although there is an option to use two temporary folders Adobe Audition will happily work with just one. Set a limit on how much space you need to reserve on these physical disks using the reserve free value.

Undo

One of the most important features of Adobe Audition is the ability to enable the user to recover from a series of edits. Only switch off the undo function if you find that you have to wait a while for very large files. Set a minimum number of undo levels here, default value is 5 but bear in mind that each level takes more physical memory and time. The Purge Undo frees up disk space by removing all temporary files and is non-recoverable.

Delete Clipboard Files on Exit

Adobe Audition can copy a large amount of data to it's clipboard files. By default these are deleted on exit. Remove this checkmark if you plan to copy wavedata to another program that is unable to start while Adobe Audition is running.

Force Complete Flush Before Saving

Older PC's with very slow hard disks sometimes have a problem when a file is written back over a file that is already open. This option was created to allow users to overcome this difficulty. Normally it should remain unchecked.

3 Colours settings

If you find that Adobe Audition defaults are getting on your nerves then use the options in this dialog to change the default colours.

4 Display settings

Spectral Display

Adobe Audition offers two ways of viewing waveforms; as amplitude over time or as frequency over time. Always time is the X (horizontal) axis leaving amplitude as a long series of tall lines extending away from the axis. In a spectral display bandwidth takes the place of amplitude with the lower frequencies closest to the X axis. Strong frequencies are shown as bright colours. The options in the spectral display drop down box are all differing algorithms dictating how the spectral data is displayed. If you have a technical or scientific mind you may explore these although a complete description is outside the scope of this book. For general purposes the default Blackmann-Harris is fine.

Resolution

This value sets the number of vertical bands used in the spectral display. The default 256 is fine for most purposes.

Window Width

Adjust this setting to 65% or 70% if you require a higher resolution along the X axis (time line)

Figure 11.3
Display settings

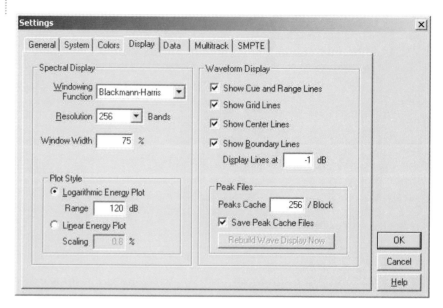

Plot Style

Spectral data can be viewed in one of two ways;

- Logarithmic, in which case the colours of the plot change according to their amplitude
- Linear when the colours represent a percentage of the overall plot. Linear plotting can be useful when mastering if you wish to see whether your mix is a little bass heavy or if you want to compare two waveforms before and after an edit.

Scaling Factor

Use this setting to concentrate on or highlight particular frequency ranges in the plot.

Waveform Display

These options for cue and range lines, grid etc. do not affect the performance of Adobe Audition and can be set according to personal preference. Boundary lines should always be seen as these two lines running horizontally along the top and bottom edges of the waveform indicate the point at which the amplitude of the waveform exceeds the ability of the soundcard to process data. This is called clipping and produces distortion. Soundcards with less headroom may benefit if you drop the display line margin from the default to -2 or even -3dB. This will provide you with an artificially low boundary to ensure that your waveform cannot clip.

Peak Files

Adobe Audition creates a temporary marker file called a Peak file (.pk) each time a fresh waveform is edited. The function of the peak file is to enable the program to load waveforms very quickly.

Peaks Cache

This is the amount of data in MB used when creating peak files. Older systems with less RAM may benefit if this value is raised to 1024MB.

Save Peak Cache Files

If space is an issue on your system you may wish to disable this option. Leave this option checked for performance benefits.

Rebuild Wave Display Now

For diagnostic use only. Rescans the loaded waveform to recreate the peak file.

5 Data settings

Embed Project Link data for Edit Original functionality

This setting links Mixdown files with associated session files.

Auto Convert All Data to 32 Bit upon opening

Check this box if you wish to convert every file to 32bit upon opening. Has a performance hit and enlarges temporary files but has the benefit of enabling much greater headroom while editing.

Interpret 32bit PCM .wav file ...

Syntrillium knew how to write a program but could have used some help with naming those options! If you happen to have an old copy of Cool Edit Pro around or some waveforms edited with an early version of Cool Edit Pro then you may wish to check this option to ensure maximum compatibility.

Dither Transform Results

In early versions of this program a 'transform' was another term for an effect. This changed with later versions but the rename never made it as far as this option.

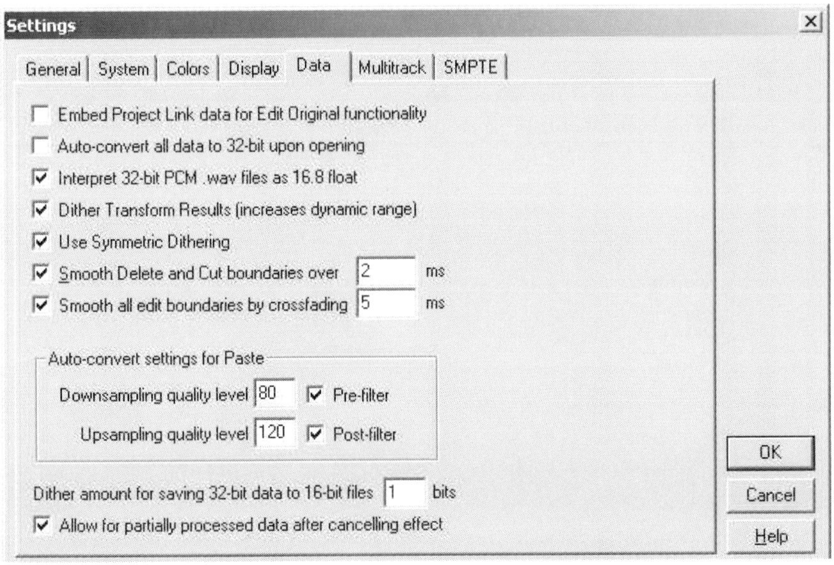

Figure 11.4
Data settings

Check this box for smoother results from effects (transforms) This is almost always enabled as the results far outweigh the small amount of processing time and the introduction of noise to produce the smoothing. However if you find that you hear tiny amounts of white noise at the end of a very long reverb trail you may wish to remove this option.

Use Symmetric Dithering
For diagnostic use only. Should remain checked.

Smooth Delete and Cut boundaries
Adobe Audition will smooth the edges of any cuts in the waveform to remove pops and clicks that occur when a waveform ends with a sample that has a greater amplitude than 0. This option should remain checked.

Smooth All Edit Boundaries by Crossfading

Adobe Audition will also gently introduce effects to the waveform to reduce pops and clicks. The amount of crossfade can be set using this value in ms. If you have a waveform that starts abruptly you may wish to reduce this value to ensure that the entire waveform sees the effect.

Auto Convert Settings For Paste
Adobe Audition is able to convert wavedata originating from other applications as it is copied from the clipboard into the edit view. The default settings can be used for most applications. If you need to ensure maximum quality from data recorded at extremely low rates these settings can be used to increase the amount of processing. See the on-line help for a thorough explanation of these values.

Dither Amount for saving 32bit data to 16bit files
Large amounts of data must be lost when saving 32bit audio as 16bit. To retain the highest quality Adobe Audition dithers the audio as it is converted. Change this value to 0 to disable dithering or to .5 to half dither. This value should almost always be left at the default of 1.

Allow for partially processed ...
Sometimes (often late at night) you may regret applying that five second canyon reverb over the entire length of your 30 minute symphony and so press the cancel button. If you disable this option (recommended) the effect will be removed from the entire waveform. However if you leave it checked then the effect will remain up until the point when you pushed cancel and you will have to edit/undo to remove it.

6 Multitrack settings

Playback Buffer Size and Playback Buffers
Each soundcard has different requirements for buffer size. Buffers are areas of memory used when sending data to the soundcard. Normally the default setting will work fine without adjustment. However if you have an older PC or soundcard and are experiencing difficulties when playing back a multitrack session you can

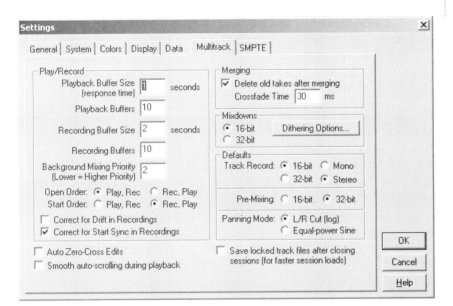

Figure 11.5
Multitrack settings

raise this setting until multitrack playback is satisfactory. The default setting is 1.5 seconds. Playback buffers deliver data to the sound card. The number of buffers is set at 10 by default. Lower this value if you have problems with an older PC.

Recording Buffer Size and Recording Buffers

These values can also be adjusted for the multitrack session. The default Buffer size is 2 Seconds with 10 Recording Buffers.

Tip

Each time a change is made to a waveblock in a multitrack session Adobe Audition must completely re-render that session in memory, creating another temporary file. This process is called Background Mixing. The Background Mix gauge on the multitrack display shows how far this process has to go. Normally it's best to wait a few seconds until background mixing has completed. If you have a complex session and playback while Background Mixing is in process you may find dropouts and skipping in playback. This can appear to be the same problem as with a buffer size issue however it is not. Wait for Background Mixing to complete and try again. A Background Mixing priority can be set in the Multitrack tab within the options dialog.

Background Mixing Priority Level

If Background Mixing appears to be taking a lot of time it may be that other processes inside the PC have a higher priority than Background Mixing. You may experiment with a lower value than the default of 2 to raise the priority of this function and so speed Background Mixing. This value does have an effect on the performance of the PC so try a few smaller values to raise the priority gradually. You may use increments of .1 (eg: 1.7 1.6 etc.)

Open and Start Order

Older soundcards may need to be told in which order to open ports or devices in the card. This setting is automatic for any card newer than a few years old and is included for backwards compatibility only. See the online help for examples for certain cards.

Correct for Drift In Recordings

Some older soundcards have different internal clocks for playback and record. In multitrack mode this can cause a problem as recordings may be made at a different rate than playback. This may cause timing drift. Enabling this option causes Adobe Audition to compare sampling rates and correct by resampling the recorded file if necessary. Default is off.

Correct for Start Sync In Recordings

Causes Adobe Audition to compare the time that the record device started with the time the playback device started. This setting ensures that record and playback start at exactly the same time. Only defeat if you need to test your soundcard in another way. The default is on.

Auto Zero-Cross Edits

Clicks and pops can be caused if a waveform is cut away from the centre line. This setting automatically causes both sides of the cut to be zero thus ensuring a noise free cut. The default is on.

Smooth Auto Scrolling During Playback

This option can be used if scrolling appears jittery during playback at the expense of some performance.

Delete Old Takes After Merging

Adobe Audition will automatically save unused takes during a multitrack session and make them available to you under the Insert Menu. This takes hard drive space and as normally you've discarded the take because it wasn't good enough it's seems better to leave this checked.

Crossfade Time

During Punch-In this is the amount of time that a crossfade will take in milliseconds. Default is 30.

Mixdown bit rate

Multitrack sessions may be recorded at 16 or 32bit. Mixdowns can be set to default at either bit rate regardless of the session bit rate. Because 32bit mixdowns can take a while this setting may be used for non-critical content.

Track Defaults

Choose to set defaults for new tracks. This can save some time when working fast in a multitrack session.

Pre-mixing

The background mixing process is usually 32bit however if you are using multiple soundcards on a complex session this setting may be used to drop the bit rate by half and speed the background mix up. May also be used if you have a slower PC with smaller hard disk space.

Panning Mode

During panning volumes may increase as both waveforms (right and left) are summed. Logarithmic panning works around this by attenuating each channel in turn. Equal Power Panning sums both channels in turn. Equal Power may have the effect of causing clipping at extremes.

Save Locked Tracks after Closing Sessions

A locked track is one that cannot be changed until it is unlocked. Effects and other parameters are frozen to avoid accidental changes. This option forces Adobe Audition to render the locked tracks as individual waveforms and save them on closing so that the session will reload faster. Locked tracks are an overhead to Adobe Audition and will cause performance issues if more than two or three tracks are locked. If you are sure enough that a track can be locked then it's probably a good idea to make a mixdown file of that track anyway and save the resources. Default is on.

SMPTE settings

Lead time to prepare wave driver

This is the delay in milliseconds before Adobe Audition starts to play or record after receiving the SMPTE start time. The function is to allow the operating system time to catch up. Fast systems should have no trouble operating at the default of 200ms.

Stopping time..

When no SMPTE is detected Adobe Audition will generate a stop event. This value is the delay in milliseconds that Adobe Audition will wait until deciding that SMPTE has truly stopped. Raising this value can be useful if the SMPTE code is erratic or contains dropouts but raising it too far will cause delays.

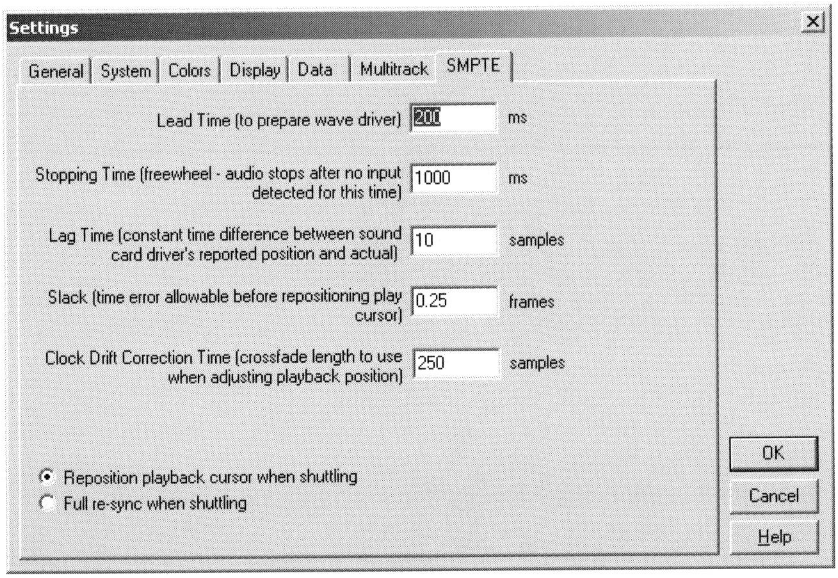

Figure 11.6
SMPTE settings

Lag time...

This value can be used to compensate if the sound card driver consistently drops behind by a fixed number of samples. The default value is ten. Values may be positive or negative numbers.

Slack Time...

Errors present in SMPTE code can cause timing problems. This value is the amount of headroom (in frames per second) that Adobe Audition will handle before taking corrective action. This setting can be very useful when dealing with code received from old tape which may have numerous dropouts. High values may cause playback or recording to stutter as Adobe Audition attempts to reposition itself with time code. The default value is 1 but as setting of 2.5 is acceptable.

Clock Drift Correction ...

This value is the number of samples used during crossfades that occur when repositioning after a correction. Higher values may be used to smooth playback if SMPTE /MTC code is particularly poor.

Reposition Playback Cursor or Full Resync

If Adobe Audition senses that it is out of sync with the time code it may take one of two actions. The first is a simple reposition of the cursor. If repositions are infrequent and slight a simple reposition may be the best option. However larger and more frequent gaps in timecode may require a full resync, This event is determined by the value of the Slack time. Raise the Slack time value if frequent repositioning is occurring.

System settings may be returned to at any time. Many users find that they experiment with system settings a good deal during the first few days of running the software but that after a short while these settings are hardly ever revisited, if at all. Modern computers have many more times processing power than is necessary to render a few waves in multitrack view and so many people may never need to change from the default settings.

Options > Device Properties

> **Hint**
>
> The ratio between audio buffer size and file buffer size is critical for optimising the performance of your PC. Experiment with different settings depending on the resources of your system. In general Total Buffer Size should be around 1 second using around 10 buffers. If you experience breakup or skipping in audio playback try reducing the number of buffers. The default setting is 10. If you experience dropouts while recording in multitrack view try increasing the buffer size to 2 or 4. The default setting is 1.

Device Properties tabs

Wave Out (Figure 11.7)	Device preferences. Playback Preferences. Edit View preferences
Wave In (Figure 11.8)	Device Preferences. Record preferences. Edit View preferences
MIDI Out (Figure 11.9)	Shows selected devices and device order
MIDI In (Figure 11.10)	Shows selected devices and device order
Ext Controller (Figure 11.11)	External Controller devices and preferences

Properties for installed devices are found using Options>Device Properties (F4).

Wave Out

Properties for playing back waveforms are found in this tab. Adobe Audition receives information regarding installed devices from the Windows operating system and displays those devices in the Device Properties dialog. All correctly

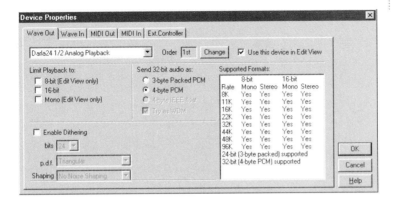

Figure 11.7
Wave Out. All correctly installed devices
appear in a drop down list.

installed devices appear in a drop down list. For waveforms in the Edit View to play-back as expected, the default playback device for the Edit View must be selected in this dialog. To select the default playback device choose the Wave Out tab and select the required device from the drop down list with the mouse. Ensure that a checkmark appears next to 'Use this device in Edit View'. If not click once in the empty box to identify the selected device as the default device in Edit View. The device order is also indicated in this tab. As each device is selected a number indicating order of preference is shown. Devices selected as 'unused' in Device Order are shown as having an order of 0. Change Device order by pressing the Change button in this tab. If your sound card does not support playback of 32bit files it is possible to limit playback to 16bit, 8bit or even mono using the options in this dialog. For playback of 32bit files while limited to 16bit playback enable dithering. Dithering increases the dynamic range while playing back as 16bits. This dialog also provides information about the capabilities of your sound card.

It's not necessary to set these options every time Adobe Audition is loaded as the software remembers the settings.

Wave In

Options for recording devices are set in the Wave In tab. Select the default Edit View recording device in the same way as the default playback device. Multiple out sound cards introduce varying amounts of latency (delay) when recording (depending on the card) and this may cause timing errors in multitrack playback.
e.g: My Echo Darla 24 card has a latency of 3ms

> **Tip**
>
> If your system has multiple sound cards yet does not behave as expected in Edit View check the default devices for Edit View in Options>Device Properties.

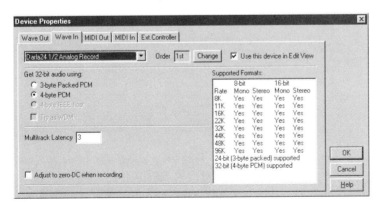

Figure 11.8
Wave In. Options for recording devices are
set here.

Calculating multitrack latency

To test for latency patch the output of your sound card to the input and load a waveform into a new session. Arm another track for record and set Adobe Audition recording. The aim is to record the output of the playback into the free track using your soundcard as a patchbay. When you have two or three seconds of the new waveform recorded place the playback cursor over an area of the wave and zoom in to sample level. By comparing the two tracks at this close level it should be possible to see and calculate any latency using the Offset feature in Multitrack View.

1   In the Multitrack view record a metronome beat using a sharp sound such as a drumstick click. Set this track to output one in the track controls.
2   Route the output of your sound card to the input using a patch cable. Be sure to mute the monitor outputs in your sound card controls to avoid damaging your equipment. The intention is to play track one and record the result to track two so ensure that device order (Options>Device Order) are set correctly.
3   Arm track two by pressing the R button in track controls and record a few seconds of the output of track one to track two
4   Set the playback cursor at the front of one of the clicks and use the Zoom To Selection button to zoom right in to the point where the beginning of each click is clearly visible.
5   Right click over the waveblock in track two and choose Waveblock Properties from the right click menu. Adjust the offset until the waveforms line up exactly. The difference between the offset value before and after adjusting is the amount of latency. Move to Settings>Device Properties>Wave In and enter this value in the latency box.

MIDI Out

Adobe Audition provides limited MIDI functionality restricted to playback of MIDI files type 0 and 1 and MIDI triggering. All MIDI devices available to Adobe Audition are listed in this tab. As with wave devices it is necessary to choose the device preference order when the software is run for the first time. Adobe Audition is able to act as a SMPTE master device for controlling of other equipment and to be controlled by SMPTE code transmitted by other equipment. Time code is transmitted using via the MIDI devices. Use this dialog to specify the MIDI output for time code.

Figure 11.9
MIDI Out. All MIDI devices available to Adobe Audition are listed in this tab.

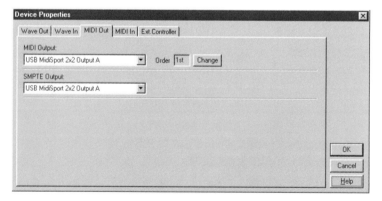

MIDI In

Choose the default device for reception of MIDI commands and time code in this dialog.

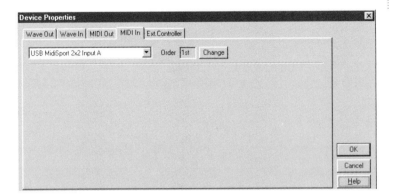

Figure 11.10
MIDI In. Choose the default device for reception of MIDI commands and time code here.

Ext. Controller

Choose which external controller will be used to control Adobe Audition. As supplied by Adobe the software has config files for the following devices;

Mackie (model unknown)
Tascam US224
Tascam US428
Event EZBus
Syntrillium Red Rover

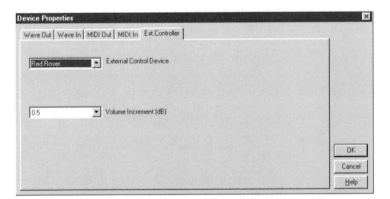

Figure 11.11
Ext. Controller. Choose which external controller will be used to control Adobe Audition.

Options > Device Order

Device Order tabs

Playback Devices (Figure 11.12)	Select playback devices from all installed devices list and set order preference
Recording Devices (Figure 11.13)	Select record devices from all installed devices list and set order preference
MIDI Output Devices (Figure 11.14)	Select MIDI output devices and order
MIDI Input Devices (Figure 11.15)	Select MIDI input devices and order

If the host system has more than one sound card or a sound card with multiple outputs it is necessary to choose the order in which Adobe Audition lists the output devices in Multitrack View. This order is purely for convenience; Adobe Audition

Figure 11.12
Playback devices

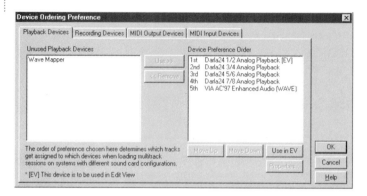

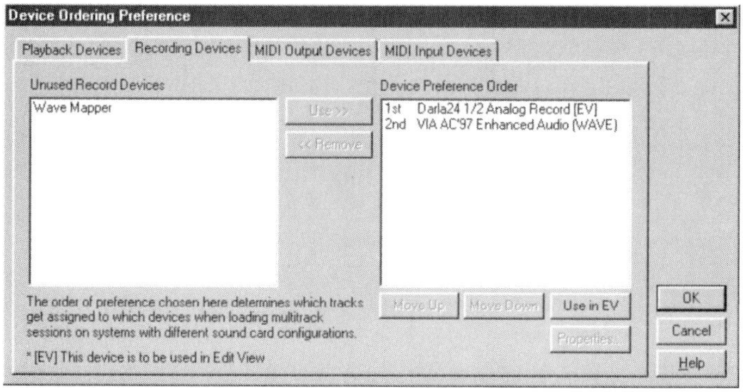

Figure 11.13
Recording devices

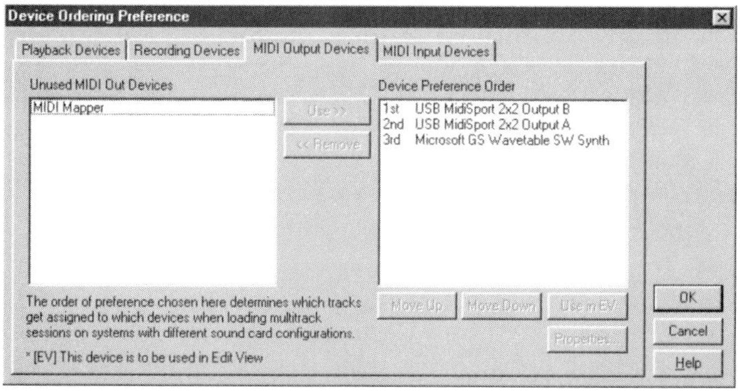

Figure 11.14
MIDI Output devices

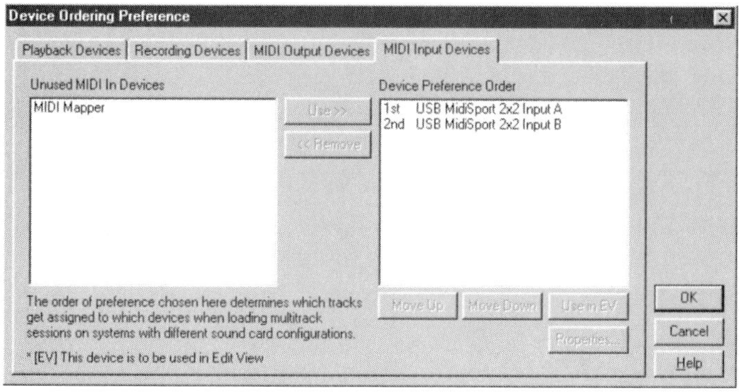

Figure 11.15
MIDI Input devices

doesn't prioritise using this list. The Device Order dialog enables these devices to be listed in order of preference. Additionally, in the event of a multitrack session being exported to Adobe Audition running on another computer and sound card system the device order will dictate which tracks are played back on which devices.

Useful things to do and know about Adobe Audition

Undo and auto-recovery

Like any large document or file it's a good idea to save your work as you are going along and especially just before making any destructive production decisions such as EQ or dynamics etc. in the Edit View. Adobe Audition has five levels of undo and even after that your waveform isn't overwritten until the save option is chosen. Settings for Undo are in the System tab in Options>Settings. More than 5 levels of undo can be set and if necessary the undo files may be purged in this dialog. Purging is only necessary if a very large effect created an undo file that was preventing normal use of the computer.

Occasionally you may find that your changes cannot be undone in this way and you wish the file to be as was before the edits were applied. In this case choose File>Revert To Saved. Revert To Saved reloads the loaded waveform from the saved file removing both the changes you don't like and the changes you may want! It's a good idea to save every time you think that you are going in the right direction.

Adobe Audition is one of the few audio applications to feature reliable auto-recovery. Computer crashes are inevitable but if Adobe Audition or the supporting operating system should crash Adobe Audition will attempt (usually successfully) to rebuild the session or loaded waveform using the data stored in the temp file location. A dialog will immediately offer the option to continue the next time Adobe Audition is started. If you don't wish to continue from where you left off or if you think that some effects or EQ settings may be causing the software to crash choose delete to return the session to the last saved state.

Real time disk space information

Adobe Audition indicates the amount of time taken and memory used on your hard disk in the Status bar underneath the Meter Display. Right clicking over this area, produces a context menu offering time in kilobytes, minutes, seconds, and fractions of a second. For best results choose to display the following data.

Data under cursor
Sample format
File Size as data in kilobytes (K)
Space remaining as time (T)

> **Tip**
>
> Save the session immediately after restoring a crashed session then close and restart Adobe Audition before resuming. This enables Adobe Audition to clean up any large temporary files. Some users report that this procedure seems to lessen the reoccurrence of Adobe Audition 'crashes' during a busy session.

Figure 11.16

`-13.2dB @  0:02.611    44100 · 16-bit · Mono    350 K    969:03.695 free`

Recommended platforms

Adobe Audition is designed to work with the following operating systems:

Windows 95
Windows 98
Windows 98SE
Windows ME
Windows NT
Windows XP
Windows 2000

Basic waveform shaping and editing can be performed on even the most low powered of machines but if you wish to take full advantage of the extremely powerful multitrack functions you will need a 1ghz processor or faster and at least 512MB of memory. Digital audio and video are resource hungry. Use only multimedia ready fast IDE or Serial ATA hard disk drives. Serial ATA is currently the preferred choice as this technology offers data rates of 100MB/s or more over a standard PC bus. USB or ZIP drives are not suitable for digital audio and video production.

Adobe Audition has been fully tested with Windows 9x / 2000 / XP operating systems. Windows 2000 and XP users should use large capacity hard disks formatted as FAT32 for greater performance. Adobe Audition is highly stable in Waveform editing mode but reliability problems may occur if multiple effects and buss are used when rendering multiple waveforms in the multitrack view. If possible ensure that video and soundcard drivers are digitally signed by Microsoft. Always ensure that your system is fully patched with the most recent service packs and critical updates provided by Microsoft. Some users report greater reliability in lower video resolutions (max 1024 x 768). Virus checking software can slow down data transfer inside your PC. In some situations it may be necessary to turn off real time virus protection. If you do this you must re-enable your virus software as soon as possible. It may be prudent to disconnect your PC from 'always on' internet cable modems or ISDN equipment while virus protection is disabled. Only disable virus protection as a last resort.

If your system suffers repeated crashes during in multitrack mode you may wish to consider defragmenting your hard disk using third party disk maintenance software or the Microsoft defragmentation utility found in the properties dialogue when right clicking on any physical device in 'My Computer' or Windows Explorer. During large projects you may wish to disable or remove any non essential processes such as scanners, system utilities, screensavers, schedulers, desktop themes, etc. Cover mount applets and gadgets all help to consume the memory and the resources you need to throw those 50mb waveforms around. Poorly written software often has memory leaks, which can continue to drain resources even after the program has been closed. Internal modems should be replaced with an external model as some audio software may detect the internal modem and attempt to install it as a sound card. Wave adapter devices bound to internal modems will also cause problems and should be disabled if possible. Consider removing your modem and replacing it with a network adapter for connection to a second computer over a local area network (LAN). Professional users often have two or more PC's, using one for

Internet and other non AV use and leaving another 'lean' PC for AV. Save energy and space by using a KVM (Keyboard Video Mouse) switch box to connect one monitor, mouse and keyboard to both computers. Be prepared to periodically rebuild the DAW from the bottom up and always keep backups of data. This is the model I use and in my experience represents the best of both worlds.

At time of writing Adobe Audition is only distributed for Windows operating systems. There are no distributions yet available for Mac, OSx, BEOS or Linux. (sorry if you already bought the book)

Preparing your PC for Adobe Audition

If you don't want to buy a brand new PC to run Adobe Audition you can find a lower specification PC and upgrade the memory or processor. However, each upgrade will have a slightly different effect. For instance upgrading the video card can't speed up the processor and so enable more effects but it will help the program to work faster. Upgrade the entire system periodically if you are able to. If not, use the following table as a guideline when deciding where best to spend your money.

Upgrade	For
Processor	More effects, EQ and faster system performance. Adobe Audition is able to deliver up to 128 tracks of multitrack audio but remember that as your session increases in complexity so the hit on your system will increase many times too. To deliver the maximum amount of tracks and effects use track locking, apply effects and amplitude envelopes permanently to waveforms wherever possible and always wait for background mixing to complete.
Hard disk	More storage, faster background mixing.
RAM	More performance, faster background mixing. Note that on most systems adding RAM above 256MB will not produce significant benefits for background mixing or performance. However upgrading RAM on a smaller system (from 64mb to 128mb for example) can lead to a much more satisfactory experience. YMMV.
Video card	Faster display, faster spectral view performance.
Mainboard	Better background mixing. Upgrade for overall system performance.

Memory

128MB – 512MB for optimum performance

Pack your PC with as much memory as you can afford at the time. Extended memory under 256MB will allow Windows to park the swapfile in upper memory. Data stored in this way can be processed much faster than data stored on hard disk. Result is faster performance, especially in multitrack mode.

Memory problems

Users of Windows 95, 98, 98SE and ME who have more than 512MB RAM may find their systems behaving strangely. For instance you may see the following error message when attempting to open a DOS session.

There is not enough memory available to run this program. Quit one or more programs, and then try again.

This is not an Adobe Audition error but a known issue with Windows running on systems with large amounts of memory. To resolve it place the following line in system.ini

[vCache]
MaxFileCache=262144

For further information on this particular hiccup find article Q253912 in the Microsoft Product Support website.

Tip

The developers of this software do not recommend overclocking of the CPU and or the mainboard.

Disabling non-essential programs at startup

Developers try and ensure that software is as easy to use as possible. This often means starting parts of the software when the machine boots. Sometimes these startup items can remain even after the software has been removed properly. Keep a track on your startup items by regularly checking the contents of your win.ini and system.ini configuration files.

Go to Start Button/Control Panel/Run. Type MSCONFIG in the Run box and press enter. The application that appears is the Microsoft System Configuration Utility. Click the startup tab and look at all the processes that start when your computer boots – even before you choose to run any software. Programs such as Real Audio (Real Audio systray etc.), Winamp, Windows Task Scheduler, Adaptec DirectCD, etc. place entries in the startup list. Remove items carefully from the list by removing the tick next to each item. Disable one at a time and restart the system each time to monitor the effect. If you find your system doesn't behave as expected you can recall the default settings by enabling the 'Normal Startup' option on the first tab within MSCONFIG.

If you can, tune your PC before installing Adobe Audition as the installation routine will automatically tune the software to your system. Adobe Audition will perform and render even in a surprisingly small system. However the seamless experience some users require is something that even the best software simply can't deliver from an older computer. Take a critical look at your computer, hardware and operating system before deciding that Adobe Audition isn't performing as you expect.

Tweaking Windows 9x

The following settings are accessible from the Control Panel of Windows 9x. Navigate to Start Button>Settings>Control panel.

Display properties

A high quality display adapter will produce an increase in system performance and reliability. Always use the latest video driver. Movie playback and record is extremely demanding on your video card. Give your system an easy time by lightening the video load. Some users report Windows GUI (Graphical User Interface) 'stopping' while using earlier versions of Adobe Audition, particularly in Multitrack View. Find the advanced tab in Display Properties and decrease Hardware Acceleration by

25% (one notch) if this is happening on your system. Display Properties may be set as follows:

- High Colour (16 Bit)
- Screen area is 800 x 600 (min) or 1024 x 768 (preferable)
- Power scheme (properties accessed through Screen Saver tab) to Always On System Standby is 'Never'
- Turn Off Hard Disks is set to '1 Hour'

Remove Auto-Insert from CD drive properties

From within the Control Panel choose the System icon. From within the System Properties dialog box choose the Device Manager tab and find your CD Drives at the top of the device list. Disable Auto Insert Notification for any CD drives. Some users remove the CD Drive completely from the workstation computer and access external drives through the LAN. However this can lead to a decrease in system performance especially if you regularly copy samples, etc. from CD.

Tune Windows automatic file system settings

Within System Properties choose the Performance tab then File System and Hard Disk buttons; Set role of this computer to Network Server to force windows to assign a higher priority to disk read and write. Set Read Ahead Optimization to maximum.

Virtual memory settings

Windows can be left to manage virtual memory settings if your system is properly equipped with enough RAM. If not, a good rule of thumb is to set Windows virtual memory settings to twice as much as the amount of physical RAM you have in your system. Physical RAM is the amount of memory (not hard disk space) that exists in the slots in your computer, 64MB, 128MB, etc.

This is a table of virtual memory settings:

Physical Memory	Virtual Memory Min	Virtual Memory Max
32	64	64
64	128	128
128	256	256
256 or more	64	64

Users with more than 128MB RAM should rely on Windows to manage virtual memory.

Tune legacy settings in system.ini

Choose; Start Button/Run. Type SYSEDIT in the Run box and press OK. When Sysedit starts look for the system.ini document. Find the section marked [vcache]. If [vcache] doesn't exist you may add it to the document beneath the section called [386Enh]. In the [vcache] section edit as follows.

Tip

Windows Active Desktop (introduced with Internet Explorer 5 and continued through Win 98) should not be enabled. Active Desktop settings are found through Start Button>Settings>Active Desktop

If your PC is connected to a network choose 'Quick Logon' from Client For Microsoft Network properties. This will speed up system startup by connecting to shared folders only on demand rather than while the system is starting.

Tip

Application software installed from a CD accessed over a LAN can work incorrectly. For best results always install software from a local CD drive

Physical RAM	MinFileCache	MaxFileCache
8	1024	1024
16	2048	2048
32	4096	4096
64	8192	8192
128	16384	16384
256	32768	32768
512	32768	32768

(with thanks to Syntrillium tech support)

If your system has more than 128MB of RAM you may find that inserting this line into the [386enh] section increases performance;

ConservativeSwapfileUsage=1

Turn off Windows system sounds

Start Button/Settings/Control Panel/Sounds. Older audio software utilities can force Windows sounds to a lower bit depth and sample rate. Adobe Audition will not do this but disabling system sounds is advisable for systems with one sound card particularly if you plan to master the waveform using an external device such as CD Writer or Minidisc recorder.

Hard disks and hard disk optimisation

During a session Adobe Audition will create temporary files in the location defined in Options>Settings>System. If the temp directory is on a different hard disk to the program directory Adobe Audition can read and write files much faster. eg:

C	8GB	System disk containing Windows files and program files	Secondary Temp Folder	C:\WINDOWS\TEMP
D	40GB	Data drive containing audio data	Primary Temp Folder	D:\cooltemp

Adobe Audition allows a reserve to be set for each drive to ensure that temporary files do not slow down system performance. Ensure that the location Windows chooses for the swapfile has enough physical space to handle both the swapfile and the Adobe Audition temporary file at the same time. Set a reserve of at least 500MB for the system partition and a more comfortable 20MB for the data partition. The Windows swapfile can easily grow to more than 200MB during a session.

Session recovery

The contents of the temporary folder are deleted automatically when the user exits the program normally. At startup Adobe Audition looks in this location and if temp files are found presents the user with a prompt asking whether the previous session should be continued or deleted. If the session is continued Adobe Audition will attempt to rebuild the session based on the information in the folder. Sometimes the temporary folder will be found to contain many temporary files, especially if sessions have closed badly or the machine has stopped etc. This folder can safely be cleared out from time to time.

To exploit the speed benefit of having two hard drive controllers the disks C and D must be physically different hard disks – not simply partitions on the same hard disk, as each disk needs a separate controller. Adobe Audition will run properly if the primary and secondary temp folders are placed in different partitions on the same disk, just not any faster. Depending on the speed of your hard disk Windows may load and run faster if the if the virtual memory 'swapfile' is written to the second disk. Defrag the system disk regularly even if the defragmentation utility declares that the drive is OK.

Wherever possible enable DMA of your hard disks to ensure high I/O speeds with little impact on your CPU. DMA removes the burden of controlling disk access from the CPU and allocates it to other devices on the mainboard. By default DMA is enabled for each drive that supports it. However this requires that DMA 'Bus Mastering' drivers are correctly loaded for your mainboard. To check the DMA state of your hard disks go to system properties and view the settings tab for each of your hard disks in the 'Disk Drives' subtree. DMA should be enabled. If not and you know that your hard disks and system support this, refer to the documentation that was supplied with your hardware. Mainboards using Intel 430FX,HX,VX,TX or 440FX,LX,EX,BX,GX will support bus mastering as well as those using the VIA chip set. (Source: D. Glen Cardenas. Jose Maria Catena ProRec.com 31.01.01). Windows 95 (osr2), Windows 98, 98SE, ME and NT (Service Pack three and above) support DMA Bus Mastering.

Removable storage

Waveforms and sessions may be archived onto removable media such as Zip and Jaz drives but removable media should not be used to store waveforms during a multitrack session as removable media does not offer the fast access times necessary for background mixing. WAV files take an enormous amount of space (10MB per min for a stereo wav) and don't like to be zipped up with WinZip or other compression utilities.

Tips

For an incredibly detailed and invaluable reference on choosing the right sort of hard disk drive for your DAW and on optimising your computer for use as a DAW I recommend the following reference work; 'SCSI vs. IDE' by D. Glen Cardenas and Jose Maria Catena (http://www.prorec.com)

Avoid combining CDROM and Hard Disks on the same EIDE channel as doing so may slow down your hard disk access speed.

Store data files at the beginning of the disk

If your older system has just one hard disk drive and getting another is right out of the question you can see increased performance if you adapt an old network administration trick to ensure that the files needing fast access (the data files) are stored at the beginning of the disk. This is achieved by using a third party utility such as Partition Commander to partition a new disk into three areas. The first area will contain system boot files, the second for audio data and the third for Windows system files. The system will start from the boot partition but find system files at the 'back' of the disk on the third partition. Meanwhile the large audio files requiring fast access speed are stored in the second partition closer to the read/write head. When installing Windows do not accept the defaults but specify an alternate location for the Windows folder. This inexpensive trick can provide significant benefits for older systems but is best applied on a brand new or recently rebuilt system as moving files around on a very full disk is time consuming and somewhat risky.

User beware! Bear in mind that nearly every piece of software is built expecting the system software to be placed in drive (or partition) C. Changing this can lead to unexpected problems and should only be attempted by users experienced in (or who enjoy) troubleshooting software problems! (or underpaid and over burdened network administrators) YMMV.

Choosing a sound card

The sound card is the physical device that sits in the back of your PC with connections for microphones, mixers and assorted input and output devices. The sound card has two main functions. The first is to detect and digitise soundwaves and pass the digital information on to applications (programs) inside the computer. Secondly the soundcard must be able to receive digital information from applications inside the computer and turn that information back into analogue (voltage) in order for it to be amplified by speakers or other devices. These two functions nearly always have to happen at the same time and more importantly, they have to appear to happen without delay. In other words we expect to hear the sound of our keyboard or guitar through the computer speakers exactly as we are performing, with no delay.

Our ears are incredibly sensitive to timing changes, and delays of less than a few milliseconds can ruin our sense of music. In computer terms this delay is called latency, measured in milliseconds. Latency is the time it takes for an event (musical note, speech, etc.) to pass through the computer, be recorded and come out again. Latency is always present and needs to be managed if your recording is going to be a satisfactory experience. Above all it makes sense to buy the most powerful and efficient soundcard that you can if you plan to make digital music into more than just a plaything. Adobe Audition communicates digitally with the sound card using a software 'driver' provided with the card. The driver enables Adobe Audition to access each of the audio channels available on the card and also to configure itself to match the capability of the card. Adobe Audition must be able to see a correctly installed sound card before it can play or record waveforms.

The increasing variety of PC Sound cards can make choosing a suitable model into a difficult decision. Typically your sound card should come from the professional end of the market and will probably not be purchased from a high street retailer. It's worthwhile not buying 'on-price' either, as budget sound cards are often 'OEM' or Other Equipment Manufacturer products. OEM products are intended for sale to computer manufacturers but often find their way into the open market at attractive prices. The main thing to be careful of with these products is that although they may look similar and are almost always called by the same name as the full price product they very often have different chipsets and even features. In the worst case this can mean that drivers are either unavailable, very difficult to get hold of, may not work without additional software or may not be updated to enable legacy products to function with new operating systems. These troubles are rare in the professional end of the market. You will pay more but money spent is repaid in time and trouble saved. When purchasing from an advertiser or on-line look for the tell-tale 'OEM' or 'Retail product' identifiers. If these are not available and the price is below what you are expecting then the product is almost certainly OEM. It's always worth a phone call before buying.

Professional sound cards from respected manufacturers such as M-Audio, Digidesign, Echo, Emagic, Creamware, etc. offer high quality results and little trouble in installing etc. Ideally your card should have multiple outputs up to about four pairs and if possible multiple inputs too. Each channel is paired as left and right creating an eight-channel card from four stereo pairs. Digital I/O is almost indispensable, especially if you intend to master onto external digital equipment such as DAT or MiniDisc. Breakout boxes allow connections to be made to a box fitted

Tip

Fit the sound card before installing Adobe Audition so the software can configure itself to the card on installation.

to the outside of the computer and avoid stress on the usually smaller connections available to PCI cards so are generally more reliable. Devices with front panel boxes such as the Creative SoundBlaster Live! Platinum series look great but require the front panel to be fitted internally and also have resource implications owing to the large number of internal devices.

Fitting more than one sound card into a PC is possible although for best results choose retail products from manufacturers with well-written drivers. Products by Echo and other manufacturers are able to synchronise so enabling three or four cards to be used at a time. In general it is best to fit the card with the most internal devices (always the professional multitrack card) first, allowing it to install completely before adding the less heavy or stereo device. Many mainboards feature integrated sound cards that should be disabled through the CMOS settings page available on system startup. Some cards are designed only to work with a particular range of resources, well written drivers enable either the resource range to be modified or for the resource to be shared with other devices.

- When installing multiple sound cards in one PC remove all cards except the primary video adapter and install the most resource intensive card first.
- Aim to install the main sound card into PCI slot 4, 3 or 2 for best performance. Install away from PC power supply and CPU but avoid installing in the last PCI slot as often the last PCI slot has difficulty properly detecting cards.
- Always reboot the system and allow the card to install normally before attempting to install the second card.
- After installing the second sound card install all other cards one at a time, rebooting between installations.
- Where possible use sound cards from the same manufacturer. Some manufacturers enable syncing of sound cards to provide multiple additional outputs/inputs in this way.

Most modern motherboards contain built in devices such as NIC's (Network Interface Card), modem and sound. All these devices use system resources and may need to be disabled if other devices are installed later on. Settings for these built in devices are found in the computer 'CMOS' (Complementary Metal Oxide Semiconductor) memory, usually under the heading 'Built In Peripherals'. This area of the computer is only available as the system boots up, either by pressing F2 or Del while the manufacturer's logo appears. CMOS settings are only available before the operating system is loaded and cannot be accessed from within Adobe Audition. Warning. Casual editing of CMOS parameters can render your computer unusable. If in doubt consult a qualified technician.

ASIO

ASIO (Audio Stream Input Output) is a specification created by Steinberg that defines the interface manufacturers of soundcards must use to allow software access to all input and output devices on a card. It was developed in an attempt to enable (as far as possible) real time monitoring of audio when using a PC soundcard. However Adobe Audition does not route digital audio through the software itself, rather it simply 'listens' to audio appearing at the inputs of the soundcard therefore it does not require the use of ASIO drivers.

MIDI OX

Sometimes it's useful to see just what MIDI information (if any) is being handled by the PC. MIDI OX provides a peek at the real time MIDI data input and output and is essential if you need to troubleshoot MIDI on your PC: http://www.midiox.com.

Figure 11.17
MIDI OX provides a peek at the real time MIDI data input and output.

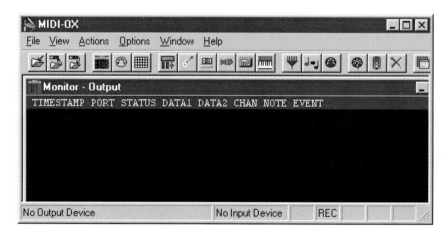

Further explanation of digital recording and reproduction

Digital recording isn't an easy thing to get your head around. After all, how can the computer make sound? What happens to a sound wave when it meets the sound card? Rather than looking at a complex waveform when trying to explain this, try creating a waveform from scratch, without recording anything.

1 Choose File>New and create a new waveform file at 8000,Mono with a 8bit resolution.
2 Place the playback cursor at the beginning of the empty waveform and use the Zoom to Selection button to zoom right in as far as possible.
3 Trick Question! It's impossible because there is nothing to see in the empty waveform.
4 Zoom to full and choose Generate>Silence from the Generate menu.
5 Generate two seconds of silence.
6 Zoom to selection again to see the individual samples. There are 8000 samples in a second of time in this waveform. Each sample has a value of 0 so the sound card would interpret this as being 'silence' and make no noise.
7 Use the mouse to drag the first square up to meet the −3db line. It's easier to see if you use the sample option in the Time Display window.
8 Now zoom to full again and press the play button. You'll hear a click as the sample is reproduced at −3db.
9 This is all that a waveform is; a series of clicks. Clicks that are closer together have a higher frequency because there are more of them per second.

More clicks per second = higher frequency = higher pitch or note.

Clicks can also be loud or quiet depending on how close they are to the centre line. This is how the waveform has dynamic range. Clicks above the line have positive phase, clicks below the line have negative phase.

The process is reversed for sound going into the sound card. The sound card ADC (Analog Digital Converter) is running all the time, like a camera with a never ending reel of film. The shutter on the camera opens and closes at a set frequency. Sound detected as analogue voltage at the input of the sound card is captured and a digital record (a sample) is made of the strength of the voltage. The amplitude information from thousands of these samples added together creates the waveform. The number of samples that can be heard because they are above 0db (silence) in every second create the pitch or note.

To sum; Sound itself isn't sampled by the sound card, a reproduction of the sound is created using information collected as the original went by.

Glossary

Auto cue

Automatically creates cue ranges based on amplitude information in the waveform.

Auto play

In the Cue List and File Open dialog boxes will play the contents of a wave file before the file is actually loaded.

Background mixing

The process of rendering a stereo wav from the information in the waveblocks and effects racks, etc. in the Multitrack View

Bit depth

The number of bits used to store waveform information.

Burning

Recording a CD of your soundtrack by using the CDR drive of your computer. Called burning as the process involves using a low powered laser

Busses

Output devices for tracks in the Multitrack View. A buss may have many inputs but only one pair of outputs. Used in place of grouping mixer tracks.

CD controls

Transport (stop, playback, etc.) for internal CD player displayed under waveform.

CD ROM

Compact Disk. Read only method of storage. Can't be overwritten but manufacturing method means data is held permanently.

CD-R

Compact Disk Recordable. Used with CDR drive allows user to 'burn' data to CDR. CDR can only be used once, even though software appears to remove files from CD deleted files still remain and space can't be reclaimed. CDR's must be 'closed' before disk can be read in a conventional CD drive. CDR is suitable for creating audio CDROM. CD-R can hold about 650mb or 74 minutes of audio data.

CD-RW

Compact Disk ReWritable. Can be written to and overwritten meaning that a single disk may be used many times similar to a floppy disk. However the nature of the read/write process means that a more sensitive drive (often just the home drive) must be used for the read/write process. Hence CD-RW disks are not suitable for distribution of data in any circumstance where the target drive is not known. Equally CD-RW disks are not suitable for audio data. Use CD-R when creating audio disks. Use CD-R disks intended only for audio if you intend your productions to be heard on systems anywhere outside of your control. TDK CD-RXG Audio CD-R will play on any CD player.

Channel

A waveform may have one or two channels. Mono waveforms have one channel, stereo waveforms have two channels. Channels may be copied from a stereo waveform by clicking the extreme upper or lower edge of the channel before clicking and dragging. To convert a stereo waveform to a mono waveform use 'Convert Sample Type'

Clipping

Garbage data created by the soundcard when the input levels exceed the soundcards ability to convert amplitude into data. Typically 0dB

Cue list

List of cues created in Edit View. Each cue is intended to identify a significant point in the waveform.

Cue marker

Identifies placement of cue in Edit or Multitrack View. Usually seen as yellow handle above and below waveform display.

DAW

Digital Audio Workstation

Direct X

Microsoft software driver

Display adapter

Hardware device inside the computer controlling the computer monitor.

Display Range Bar

Solid green bar above waveform display in Edit View. The length of the bar illustrates the amount of the waveform seen in the current view.

Display Time Window

Window beneath the waveform view with constantly updated figure showing elapsed time in a number of formats.

Drop down box

List box which expands when clicking over small handle to right of box.

DSP

Digital Signal Processor. The PC doesn't have any hardware devoted to DSP in an audio sense but this term is used to describe effects that have been created digitally rather than in the analogue domain.

Edit View

Two channel waveform editor.

Effects

Digital effects created by Adobe Audition.

Effects Racks

Effects groups applied to single tracks in the Multitrack View.

Envelopes

Graphical illustration of pan, volume or other data over waveblocks in the Multitrack View. Envelopes can be adjusted using the mouse.

EQ

Equalisation or tone controls.

Filters

Filter out frequency ranges e.g: Graphic Equaliser, Phase Shifter.

Frequency range

Variable range of frequencies based around a centre frequency.

Handles or nodes

Small square boxes available for dragging using the mouse. Right click to see data values.

Hard drive

Physical storage device inside the computer.

Impulse

A waveform describing the characteristics of a sound that is overlaid on another waveform during convolution. The second waveform then adopts the characteristics of the first.

Level meters

Indicate amplitude data received by Adobe Audition from sound card driver.

Loops

Short section of waveform seamlessly repeating.

Menu bar

Drop down list of items.

MIDI

Musical Instrument Digital Interface. A LAN protocol adopted by the music industry for sending and receiving data between PC's.

MP3

System of encoding waveform to produce very high quality sound using extremely small file sizes. The standard for distribution of audio over the web.

MTC

MIDI Time Code. A method of sending timing information between MIDI capable devices.

Multitrack sound card

Physical hardware device inside the computer featuring more than one pair of inputs and outputs.

Multitrack View

Shows arrangements of waveblocks in tracks. Tracks are played in synchronisation and so waveblocks on different tracks can be overlaid to create multitrack audio.

Noise

White noise contains an equal proportion of all frequencies. Brown and Pink noise is weighted towards the low frequencies.

Placekeeper

A floating window used as a spacer between other windows when docked.

Play list

In the Cue List the Play List is used to play back cue ranges in a pre-determined order.

Playback cursor

Shows current position of playback in the waveform.

Plug in

Third party software utilised by Adobe Audition 1.0 through Direct X. Typically additional effects software.

RAM

Random Access Memory. Physical storage inside the computer.

Range or selected area

Selection of the waveform created by dragging the mouse over any area.

Red Rover

USB control device. Created by Syntrillium. A set of transport controls and multitrack information set into a small remote control.

Ripping
Digital extraction of audio data from pre-recorded CD's.

Ruler Bar
Calibrated ruler below the waveform display indicating time or any number of other formats.

Sampling rates
Expressed as frequency. CD quality audio is made of samples reproduced 44,100 times per second. In other words there are 44,100 individual samples in every second of waveform data at that frequency rate.

SMPTE
Society Of Motion Picture Technical Engineers. Body behind the SMPTE timecode method of synchronisation.

Snapping
Playback cursor is attracted to area of ruler bar or other choices in Edit>Snapping menu. Makes precise positioning of playback cursor much easier.

Sound card
Physical device inside the computer able to convert audio into digital data.

Spectral View
Displays waveform as frequency rather than amplitude

Status Bar
Area in the extreme lower right of the program window. Contains text fields showing data relating to available storage space, etc. Right click over this area to see more options.

Temp files
Data created by Adobe Audition at program time and stored temporarily on hard drive.

Timecode
MTC (MIDI Time Code) or SMPTE timecode is read and generated by Adobe Audition and so is able to synchronise with external machines such as VCR or reel tape multitrack machines.

Tones
Sinewave or other wave types at fixed or varying frequencies.

Toolbars
Small button bars above waveform display. Buttons duplicate menu bar items and may be removed. Right click over button bar to view options.

Track Controls

Small controls to left of each track in Multitrack View. Contains controls for output and recording device, mute solo and pan etc.

Track Properties

Volume, pan and other values available by right clicking on any free space in track controls to produce floating window or in table form through Track Mixers.

Tracks (In Multitrack View)

Waveblocks in multitrack view are laid out in tracks to enable many waveblocks to be played at the same time.

Transport bar

Button bar containing VCR style controls for controlling playback functions.

YMMV

Your Mileage May Vary. In other words the complexity and variables associated with computer systems of all sorts' means that a simple statement such as 'add more RAM for better performance' takes on extra meaning. Stuffing your old Intel 486 system with 256 MB of RAM is not going to make as much difference as upgrading your main board and processor for instance. Hence 'Your Mileage May Vary'.

Wav

Shortened term for waveform used as file name suffix in Windows.

Waveblock

Contains waveform data in multitrack view but crucially doesn't change data of source waveform. Waveblocks may be moved, deleted, trimmed etc. without affecting original recording.

Waveform

Computer representation of sound as data.

WDM

Windows Driver Model. WDM drivers are compatible across all Microsoft Windows operating systems. The object of WDM drivers is to make it much easier for vendors to develop and support their products without having to write a different driver for each Windows OS. (9x,ME,XP,2000 etc.). Adobe Audition 1.0 Version supports WDM drivers for the first time.

Appendix
Multichannel encoding within Adobe Audition

Any system with a 5.1 decoder can read and interpret files produced using the Adobe Audition Multichannel Encoder. This includes domestic and professional DVD and home theatre systems and PC's with 5.1 capable soundcards. Multichannel encoding preview is only enabled if your soundcard supports it. The multichannel encoder is able to export the loaded session in one of three ways;

* As six individually encoded wav files
* As one coded wav file suitable for postproduction
* As a complete Windows Media Player ready file

Choose View>Multichannel Encoder to produce the Multichannel Encoder dialog. Each track within the current session is imported into the dialog ready for encoding. Track names are imported from the session. The session should be complete and saved before the Multichannel Encoder is used. Before using the Encoder the mix should be complete for stereo. In other words the mix should have been defined so that playback on a regular stereo system reflects as far as possible your production choices. Attempting to produce entirely for 5.1 and ignoring the stereo picture will adversely affect your 5.1 production.

1 Left click over the first track in the Track List within the Multichannel Encoder dialog to select it.
2 From within the track options section of the dialog choose whether to use one of the preset panning options or to create your own panning envelopes using the Pan Envelopes option.
3 Repeat for each track
4 Export to one of the three export options.

Using the Pan Envelopes function

The seven fixed panning assignments provide a building block for your 5.1 production. Creating the illusion of movement for your production requires that panning envelopes for each track are created. Fortunately the interface provided by Adobe Audition for this enables dramatic effects to be produced relatively quickly.

1 Left click over any track in the Track List to select it.
2 Choose the Pan Envelopes option from within the Track Options section of the encoder.

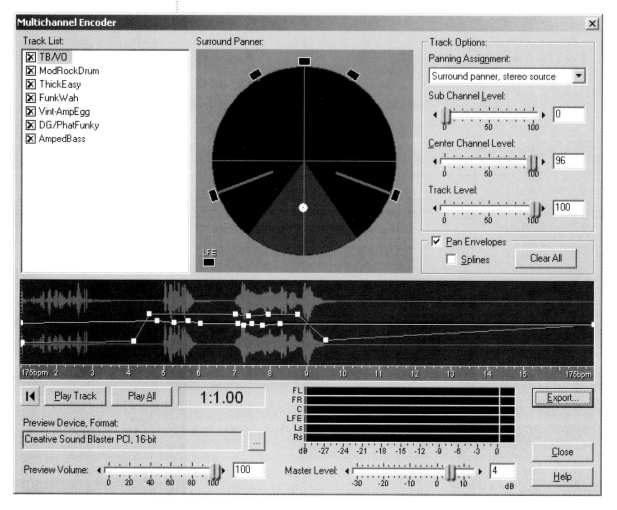

Figure A.1

As the orb is dragged around the window, nodes appear on the envelope over the waveform.

3 Left click anywhere along the X axis within the waveform display to place the cursor at any point.

4 Move the mouse cursor to the central surround panner window and click and hold the white 'orb' icon.

5 Drag the 'orb' to a suitable point within the Surround Panner window

6 Click again further along the waveform to move the cursor

7 Move the orb again to create further volume and pan envelopes.

As the orb is dragged around the window nodes appear on the envelope over the waveform. The function of the Surround Panner window is to clarify the effect of the envelopes. The listener sits at the centre of the crosshair facing the two front speakers (Fl and FR) and the centre channel or sub speaker (LFE). Behind and to the sides are two more speakers (Ls and Rs). Volume from each speaker is illustrated by a straight blue line from each speaker. The position of the stereo image is illustrated by light and dark shaded areas of the surround panner window. As the orb is moved within the window the amplitude of the speakers and therefore the sound image changes.

Previewing and exporting the 5.1 Production

The 5.1 production can be previewed from within the encoder. Previewing is important as panning decisions affect amplitude. It is essential to ensure by viewing the level meters that no part of your production could cause distortion or imbalance during playback or even performance. Preview the entire production and if necessary use the Master Level fader to attenuate the production if necessary. When the production is finished use the Export function to produce a further Export Properties dialog. The production may be exported as a complete WMA file ready for Windows Media Player on any XP system or as a wav for decoding by another method. A complete description of the encoding of professional 5.1 surround sound productions is beyond the scope of this book. However the included help files in this area are informative and contain essential advice, particularly if your production is intended for commercial presentation and should be carefully read.

Index